Colgate's
Basic
Sailing
Theory

Colgate's Basic Sailing Theory

STEPHEN COLGATE

President, Offshore Sailing School Ltd.

Illustrations: John Tubb Associates

 VAN NOSTRAND REINHOLD COMPANY

New York   Cincinnati   Toronto   London   Melbourne

Van Nostrand Reinhold Company Regional Offices:
New York   Cincinnati   Chicago   Millbrae   Dallas

Van Nostrand Reinhold Company International Offices:
London   Toronto   Melbourne

Jacket Photo by Walter Iooss, Courtesy of Sports Illustrated
Printed by Murray Printing Co.

Published by Van Nostrand Reinhold Company
A Division of Litton Educational Publishing, Inc.
450 West 33rd Street, New York, N.Y. 10001

Published simultaneously in Canada by
Van Nostrand Reinhold Limited

16   15   14   13   12   11   10   9   8   7   6   5   4   3   2   1

CONTENTS

FOREWORD

This book's successful use in conjunction with the Offshore Sailing School's basic course of instruction has prompted the publication of this edition, slightly augmented for beginning sailors everywhere. A few hours applied to its study will greatly speed up the learning process once you are aboard a boat. Sailing must be learned by doing, but it is twice as effectively learned by doing the *right* thing the *first* time.

I am going to throw a great deal of material at you at first. Don't be overwhelmed by it, because I realize most readers won't get it all the first time. The important terms will be repeated throughout the rest of the book, and, through repetition, the strange words and movements of this sport will soon become second nature.

Finally, a word about terminology. The "language of the sea" is traditional and comes from the days of square-rigged ships. Until you understand the strange words used in sailing, you will be unable to sail well. There are times on a boat when the action is fast, and the correct action has to be taken at the right time or disaster results. You can't afford to say, "Let that thing over there go!" when you mean, "Free the jib sheet!"

Happy Sailing.

Thanks to my wife, Doris, who tirelessly typed the whole manuscript.

S. C.

TYPES OF SAILBOATS

Although we will be learning here to sail a sloop (there are more sloops around than anything else), we may just as well, at this early stage, pick up the ability to tell one type of sailing craft from another. Sailboats fall into different categories based on the number of masts they have and the location of these masts.

Single-masted sailboats are either sloops, catboats, or cutters. The sloop has two sails, a jib forward of a mainsail. A catboat has no jib and the mast is near the bow. The cutter is a sloop with the mast near the center of the boat. Actually, if the mast is more than two-fifths of the waterline length aft (behind) the point where the bow emerges from the water, it's a cutter.

Double-masted sailboats are either yawls, ketches or schooners. However, in the former two, the small mast is aft the larger. The mizzen mast, as it is called, is near the stern of the boat. A good rule of thumb is if the steering apparatus (the tiller or steering wheel) is forward of the mizzen it's a yawl,

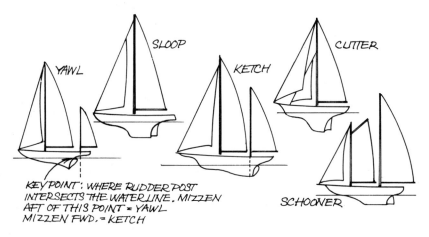

KEY POINT: WHERE RUDDER POST INTERSECTS THE WATERLINE. MIZZEN AFT OF THIS POINT = YAWL MIZZEN FWD. = KETCH

fig.1

3

and if behind the mizzen it's a ketch. There are a few instances where this guideline doesn't work. Every boat has a rudderpost that turns the rudder for steering. Where this rudderpost intersects the waterline is the real point of demarcation. If the mizzen is forward of this point, it's a ketch, if aft, it's a yawl. However, since many people don't like to steer a boat with a mast right in front of them obstructing their visibility, they have the designer arrange a steering mechanism that leads forward of the mizzen. Thus, the wheel is forward of the mizzen, the rudderpost is aft, and it's still a ketch.

If the boat has two masts and the forward mast or "foremast" is smaller or the same size as the after mast, it's a schooner. Schooners can have three, four or even more masts. None of the masts on a schooner is called the mizzen. Well, *almost* never! The largest schooner ever built was the Thomas F. Lawson, launched in 1902, with seven masts. Beginning at the bow, its masts were called the Foremast, Main, Mizzen, Frigger, Jigger, Driver and Spanker. But you'll never need to know that, so try to forget it . . .

DIMENSIONS AND PARTS
OF THE BOAT

Open any boating publication to the design section and you will find a list of dimensions for the particular design being commented upon. These are usually abbreviated.

LOA stands for "length overall." This is the total length of the boat from the bow to the stern in a straight line, not including any bowsprit.

The "load waterline" or simply "waterline length" is abbreviated as LWL. This is the straight-line distance from the point where the bow emerges from the water to the point where the stern emerges from the water.

As you can see in Figure 2, the topsides of the boat are the sides extending from the waterline up to the deck. If you hear someone say, "Look at the beautiful bright topsides on that boat," it's not just a comment on the vessel's intelligence. He means the boat has natural wood topsides that have been varnished. "Brightwork" is varnished wood trim. Another person in the cabin of a cruising boat may say, "I'm going topsides." This has nothing to do with the topsides of the boat, it means he's going up on deck, another non-sequitur of the sailing idiom.

The next common dimension of a boat is its draft (DRA). This is the distance from the water level to the deepest part of the boat. If a boat sailing along touches bottom in three feet of water, then her draft is three feet or she "draws" three feet, which is another way of saying the same thing. Centerboard sailboat designs will usually state two drafts for the boat, such as, "She draws six inches with the board up and four feet with the board down." It is obviously important to know how much your boat draws so you can look at the depth of water on a chart and avoid areas that are shallower than your draft.

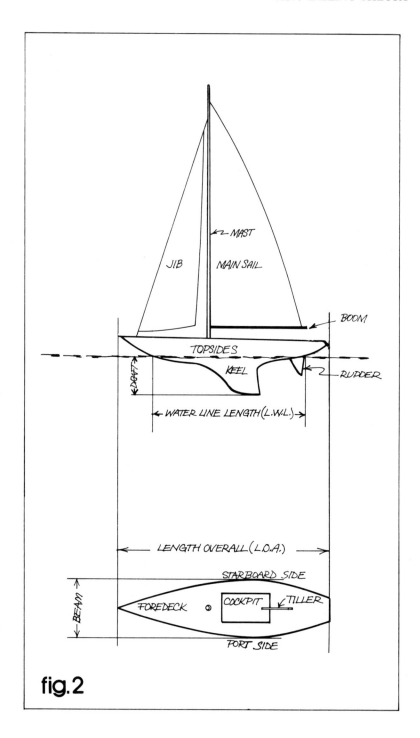

fig.2

Common advertisements in boating magazines can be incomprehensible at first, yet how could you buy a boat if you didn't know what the ads or the dealers were saying? Here is a typical ad from YACHTING magazine.

> "She has a minimal wetted surface hull, high aspect ratio keel, large separation between the CLR and rudder, and a high ballast/displacement ratio. Her trimtab is linked to separate rudder for reduced leeway and better control, and she has high aspect ratio rig with large foretriangle. The PT-40 is light enough to surf readily, yet heavy enough to carry her sail."

In short, you should understand such descriptions.

The beam of the boat (BM) is its maximum width, not its width at deck level as one might expect. Figure 3 (Ballast Displacement Ratio) shows the cross-section of a keelboat where the maximum width is about in the middle of the "topsides" (sides of the boat), so it's at that point where the beam is measured. When the topsides curve inward to meet the deck, rather than go straight up, the result is called "tumblehome." It's a weight saving device in classes of sailboats that specify a minimum beam in their rules, but allow wide design latitude otherwise.

Another term bandied about by manufacturers, salesmen and sailors is "aspect ratio" (Figure 4). Notice it was used twice in the YACHTING ad quoted, in regard to the keel and then to the rig or sails. It is the relationship of the height of anything to its breadth. If a sail is 60 feet measured along the mast and 15 feet along the boom, then the aspect ratio is stated as 8 to 1, or AR = 8. One might think this should be 4 to 1 (60 feet divided by 15 feet) and is often stated in such terms, but that would be the AR of a rectangle which has twice the average width of a triangle with the same base. So we double it and arrive at an AR of 8:1. If the same boat added five feet to her boom, she would have a lower aspect ratio -- 60 feet divided by 20 feet = 3, and this doubled equals an AR of 6 to 1. The importance of aspect ratio has to do with boat performance. A high aspect ratio sail goes better upwind whereas a low AR sail works better with the wind pushing from behind.

Another ratio stated often is the ballast-displacement ratio of a boat. This is the relationship of weight of the iron or lead "ballast" in the keel (used like a pendulum to keep the boat upright) to the total weight of the boat. For instance, if a 10,000 pound boat has 4000 pounds of lead in its keel for ballast, it has a 40% ballast-displacement ratio. The higher the ratio, the more stability the boat has. A ratio of about 50% is very good for a cruising boat.

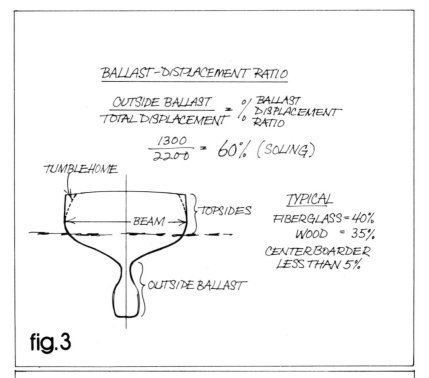

BALLAST–DISPLACEMENT RATIO

$$\frac{OUTSIDE\ BALLAST}{TOTAL\ DISPLACEMENT} = \% \begin{array}{l} BALLAST \\ DISPLACEMENT \\ RATIO \end{array}$$

$$\frac{1300}{2200} = 60\% \ (SOLING.)$$

TUMBLEHOME

TOPSIDES

BEAM

OUTSIDE BALLAST

TYPICAL
FIBERGLASS = 40%
WOOD = 35%
CENTERBOARDER
LESS THAN 5%

fig.3

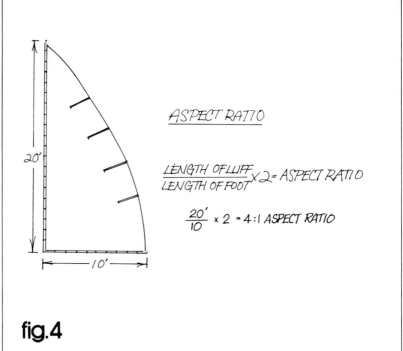

ASPECT RATIO

$$\frac{LENGTH\ OF\ LUFF}{LENGTH\ OF\ FOOT} \times 2 = ASPECT\ RATIO$$

$$\frac{20'}{10} \times 2 = 4:1\ ASPECT\ RATIO$$

20'

10'

fig.4

RIGGING AND SAILS

Now that we are able to look at a sailboat and characterize its type, the next step is to know the names of the various items of rigging and sails.

Rigging

Rigging, all the wire and line (rope) used aboard a sailboat, is broken down into two major categories -- running rigging and standing rigging.

Running rigging consists of all the lines on a boat that are easily adjusted. "Halyards" raise and lower the sails, and "sheets" adjust them in and out laterally. Halyards and sheets are the major components of running rigging and take the name of the sail to which they are attached. A main halyard

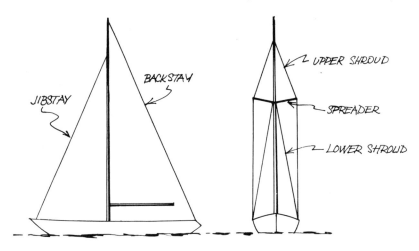

fig.5

raises and lowers the mainsail. A jibsheet adjusts the trim of the jib. At this juncture, let's clear up another possible source of confusion. The "trim" of the jib or of any sail is the angle of that sail to the wind direction at a given point in time. But to "trim" a jib is to pull it in with the jib sheet, and to "ease" or "start" it, is to let it out.

Standing rigging consists of the wires that hold up the masts of a sailboat. It too is broken down into two major categories -- "stays" and "shrouds." The stays keep the mast from falling "fore and aft" (over the bow or the stern). The shrouds keep it from falling "athwartships" (over the side of the boat.

The standing "backstay" is found on most boats and runs from the head (top) of the mast back to the deck at the middle of the stern. The stay leading forward is called the "headstay" if it leads from the head of the mast to the bow, the "jibstay" if it leads from partway down the mast to the bow, or the "forestay" if it leads to the middle of the foredeck which is the area of deck forward to the foremost mast. Many sailors use these three terms for stays interchangeably, however, so don't get too confused by them.

Because shrouds lead from the edges of the deck up to attachment points on the mast, the angle they make to the mast is more acute than that of the stays. For this reason, the shrouds that lead highest on the mast -- the "upper shrouds" -- run through the end of metal or wooden struts or tubes on either side of the mast. These tubes are called "spreaders" since they spread the angle the shroud makes with the mast. This results in better support for the upper section of the mast. It also results in compression load on the spreaders which tends to bend the mast at that point. To counteract this bend, most boats have another set of shrouds -- the "lower shrouds" -- on either side of the mast leading from the base of the spreaders to the edge of the deck. Since these originate lower down the mast, the angle they make with the mast is wide enough to eliminate the need for extra spreaders, as you can see from Figure 5.

Sails

Modern mainsails, pronounced "mains'ls", but more often called "mains," and jibs are made of Dacron, a Dupont product, in the United States. The important property of Dacron is that it stretches less than most synthetics on the market. A sailmaker cuts and sews a sail in a desirable shape. He doesn't want it to lose this shape under the pressure of the wind, so his aim in choosing cloth is to have as little stretch as possible, or at least a predictable amount.

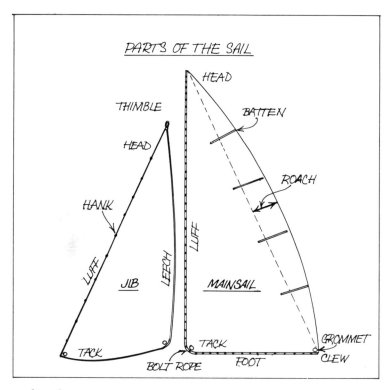

fig. 6

When completed, the sail is triangular in shape. The three edges of the sail are the "luff" -- the leading edge, the "leech" -- the trailing edge, and the "foot" -- the bottom edge. The three corners are the "head" at the top, the "tack" -- the forward lower corner, and the "clew" -- the after lower corner. Notice in Figure 6 that a straight dotted line between the head and the clew indicates that the sail is convex. The material outside this line is called "roach." If the sail were concave, as many jibs are, it wouldn't have any roach. It would still have a leech, though, since that is just the area of the sail between the head and the clew.

The foot and luff of the mainsail are reinforced by a rope called the "boltrope." This is the only rope on a boat which we do not refer to as line. The sailcloth is sewn to it, as are the sail slides that go on the sail-track on the mast of larger boats. On small boats the boltrope goes inside a groove in the mast and boom, taking the place of sail slides.

The boltrope reinforces the luff and foot, but something is needed to keep the leech of the sail from unraveling. The sailmaker sews a strip of doubled over material along the edge which is called "tabling." Sometimes he incorporates in the tabling a light line that is attached at the head and is adjustable at the clew. This is called a "leech cord" or "pucker string" and is used to reduce leech flutter which occasionally occurs along the trailing edge of the sail. Also along the leech, evenly spaced, are pockets that hold strips of wood or plastic called "battens." The purpose of the battens is to support the roach of the sail, which would otherwise flop over by gravity. A typical batten for a 25 foot boat might be 1 inch wide, 24 inches long and taper from about 1/4 inch thick to 1/8 inch thick over its length. The thin end enters the batten pocket first because it's more flexible and will have to follow the curve of the sail. There is sometimes a hole in the thick end, a carry over from the time when battens were tied in the pockets. Now the opening is from above and tying is no longer necessary.

Sails are the driving force of a sailboat and just as any engine needs care, so do sails. Sunlight deteriorates Dacron so, at least when not in use, they should be kept out of it. Dried salt from spray makes them heavy as the salt picks up moisture from the air each time out and dirt particles tend to shorten the life of the material. So sails should be washed occasionally with warm water and mild soap.

Sails should be folded before placing them in the sailbag. They have been treated with a filler to reduce porosity and stretch. Stuffing them in the sailbag breaks down the filler in the cloth and reduces its life. The sails come out of the sailbag completely wrinkled and it may take an hour or so of sailing to smooth the wrinkles out. Also, wrinkles reduce sail area. Try this experiment: Lay a piece of typewriter paper on a table and crumple up a second piece. Now, smooth out the crumpled piece and lay it down on top of the first piece, lining up the top edges. You'll probably end up about 1/16 inch short at the bottom and this is over a span on only 11 inches! Furthermore, wrinkles tend to disrupt the airflow over the sail. There's not much sense for sailmakers to do research for smoother, tighter weave cloths if the sailor messes it up with a bunch of wrinkles.

So get in the habit of folding the sails of any small boat after each sail. This obviously can't be done with the sails of large cruising boats, but the forces are larger and the wrinkles tend to "sail out" quickly anyway, so there is little need. The proper way is described in Appendix IV. Remember to make the final roll such that the clew is on the outside in the case of a mainsail and the tack is outside in the case of a jib, since these are the corners you need first respectively when putting on, or "bending on," the sails.

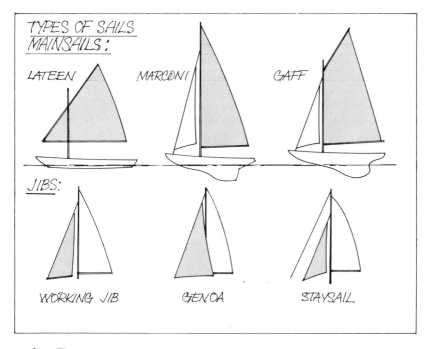

fig.7

GETTING UNDERWAY

Whether you buy or charter, rent or borrow your sailboat, it will either be tied to a float, kept out on a mooring or "drysailed" (launching it by trailer or by hoist each time you want to sail it.) The latter is much more work, but has advantages for the racing sailor. First, the bottom won't get fouled -- slime and seaweed won't have a chance to grow on it. This is more crucial in salt water than in fresh, but will definitely slow the boat down in either case. Second, the boat won't have a chance to absorb water, thereby making it heavier and slower. Even fiberglass boats are "hydroscopic" in that they absorb water. The other reasons for drysailing a boat are if mooring or docking facilities are unprotected, inadequate or unavailable.

Getting to a Moored Boat

Since most sailboats are kept at moorings, we'll direct our attention to these. When you load your dinghy to row or motor out to the moored sailboat, always step into the middle of the boat and not on the seats. The lower you get the weight in the boat, the more stable it will be, so sit down immediately before someone else attempts to step into the boat. Load the middle of the boat first in order to keep the trim level. The "fore and aft trim" of any boat is the relationship of its design waterline, which is painted on the boat, to the surface of the water. You might say a sailboat was "down by the bow" if it had too much weight (crew or equipment) forward or "dragging the stern" if it had too much weight aft. So keep the dingly level or slightly down by the stern and don't overload it.

Whoever is rowing, or running the outboard may ask you, once you are seated, to "trim the boat." This means you should ease your seat (and weight) to port or starboard so that the dinghy rides level, making it easier to row, and safer in choppy water.

"Freeboard" is the distance from the edge of the deck to the water when the boat is level. If the boat is so heavily loaded that it sinks down in the water leaving only about six inches of freeboard, any rolling by waves or shifting of passenger weight may cause the dinghy to "ship" water over the side (fill up). Before long it will sink as the weight of the water lowers the freeboard even more.

Boarding Your Boat

If your moored sailboat is a small (under 20 feet long) centerboard type, when you reach it you should step in the middle of the cockpit *and* lower the centerboard for stability.

The centerboard is a metal or wood plate that is pinned at the forward end and pivots down in an arc when lowered, as opposed to a "daggerboard" that doesn't pivot but raises or lowers vertically. The housing for the centerboard is called the "centerboard trunk." The board is usually kept in the "up" position when the boat is moored, so seaweed won't have a chance to form on it.

Since most centerboards are relatively light weight, they don't act much like a keel (a heavy fixed weight well below the surface of the water). When it is lowered, stability is improved, but crew weight on one side of the boat or the other has the most effect. Lowering the centerboard, however, slows up the rolling motion of the boat, so if you step to one side the boat won't tip so fast and you can get your balance back before the boat capsizes (turns over).

The reason for stepping into the cockpit rather than forward on the deck is again one of stability. Most planing sailboats (those that can skim the surface of the water at high speeds, much like skipping a stone) are veed in the bow and have a reasonably flat run aft. If you step in the bow you push the veed part deeper and raise the flat stable part out of the water, so the boat *has* to tip.

Getting aboard a keelboat is easier in that you don't have to be concerned with capsizing it. The launch or dinghy is usually being held next to the sailboat by an operator near the stern and a common error is for someone near the bow of the launch to get out first and let the bow drift off. Either the person in the bow of the launch should be the last off and should hold it in close for the others, or he should get onto the sailboat and hold the bow of the launch in with the "painter" (the launch's bow line).

When getting aboard make sure you don't pinch your fingers between the launch and the sailboat. If the sailboat is high-sided and there are no lifelines to grab, the safest way to board, particularly if it's rough, is to turn around, sit on the deck and then swing your legs aboard.

Setting Sail

In most types of boats the process of setting sail is fairly much the same. For the parts of the sail following, refer to Figure 6. Locate the clew of the "main" and run the foot out along the boom. The boom will either have a groove that the foot runs inside or a track which accommodates slides sewn on the foot of the sail. One person will have to feed the slides onto the track or the foot into the groove, while another pulls the clew out to the end of the boom. A pin is placed through the tack corner, the "outhaul" attached to the clew and the foot may then be stretched out tight and "secured" or cleated.

The battens are placed in the batten pockets, with the thin end entering first. Check that you have the right length in the proper pocket. Starting at the tack, follow along the luff to make sure there are no twists in the sail. Attach the main halyard, looking "aloft" (up) in case it's "fouled" (twisted) around a spreader or backstay. If the main luff has slides, put them all on the mast track starting at the head of the sail. If the mast is grooved, you will have to feed the luff of the sail in the groove as it goes up, but first get the jib ready.

The tack of the jib is the corner that is attached first. There are a number of ways to quickly identify this corner: (1) the sailmaker's label or emblem is almost always located there since there is an International Yacht Racing Union rule to this effect, (2) the angle at the tack is much wider than the angle at the head, (3) the jib hanks or snaps usually attach to the jibstay from right to left for right-handed people -- in other words, the opening in the snap is on the left. If you dump a large sail out of the bag, just by looking at one jib hank you can tell which way to follow the luff to the tack. (4) A good crew, knowing that the tack is needed first, will leave that corner on top of the sail after "bagging it" (putting it away in a sailbag). And (5) on larger boats, "TACK" is often written at the corner so there can be no mistake.

Next attach the tack and start hanking on the snaps from bottom up. If you start at the top of the sail you would have to hold the sail up and hank on each snap underneath. This would get mighty heavy after awhile. Also, the sail would be up high where a gust of wind could blow it overboard. So you start with the tack first and pull the sail forward between your legs to keep it low, protected from the wind, and to avoid draping it over the side of the bow in the water.

The jib sheets (the lines that pull the jib in and out) are now attached and led through their proper "leads" (blocks, or pulleys, that adjust the trim angle of the jib) and either a "figure-eight" knot or "stop" knot as shown in Figures 8 and 9 is made in the end of each sheet. This keeps the end of the line from running out of the jib lead when you let it go. Of the two knots, the "stop" knot is probably the more sure. Now attach the jib halyard that will pull the sail up and you're all set to go.

FIGURE EIGHT KNOT

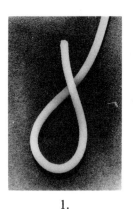  

| 1. | 2. | 3. |

fig.8

STOP KNOT

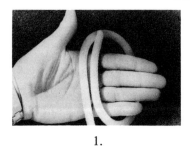 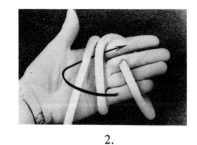

| 1. | 2. |

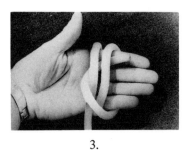 

| 3. | 4. |

fig.9

The mainsail is the first sail to raise for various reasons. It acts like a weather vane and keeps the boat headed into the wind. This is most important on a cruising boat since you are apt to motor out of a harbor, head the boat into the wind and idle the engine while the mainsail is raised. If the boat swings broadside to the wind, which might happen if you raise the jib first, the mainsail will fill with wind, press against the rigging, and bind on the sail track making it virtually impossible to raise the sail further.

The same problems arise on smaller boats, but if you start from a mooring, the boat automatically "lays" with her bow pointed directly into the wind, unless the current is strong enough to overpower the wind's effect on the boat, in which case the wind can't be strong enough to give problems in sail raising. With small boats sailing from moorings, therefore, the only reason to raise the jib last is because the jib flails around during and after raising. This tangles the jib sheets and causes an awful commotion on a windy day, which continues until the main is raised and you are underway. The flailing also reduces the life of the jib, because it breaks down the cloth fibers and fatigues the sail at the batten pockets.

ONE IMPORTANT ITEM TO REMEMBER WHEN RAISING SAILS IS THAT ALL THE SHEETS MUST BE COMPLETELY LOOSE so the sail will line up with the wind rather than fill. At the same time, all lines that might be holding the boom down, like the downhaul and boom vang, must be eased so that nothing can keep the main from going all the way up. A crew member should hold the after end of the boom up in the air to relieve the pull of the leech of the sail.

Leaving the Mooring

Before leaving the mooring, let's get a couple of basic terms clear: *starboard* and *port* are two terms in as constant use aboard a boat as *fore* and *aft*. Starboard is right and port is left. Some remember this by the fact that "port" and "left" have the same number of letters. It's been said that the words came from sailing ships of long ago that used a sweep or oar for steering. It was called the "steering board" and was over the right side of the boat when one faced the bow. Thus the right side was called the "steering board" side and later, the starboard side. The left side was clear to lay next to a dock while the boat was in port and became the "port" side.

Now we're ready to sail away, but since the boat is headed directly into the wind at a mooring and is not moving through the water, it is what we call "in irons" or "in stays." This can happen at other times when a boat attempts

to change tacks by turning into the wind, is stopped by a wave, and loses
"steerageway" or "headway." In order to steer a boat, water must be flowing
past the rudder. If the boat is "dead in the water" (motionless) the rudder is
useless, so the sails have to be used in its place.

The sails, because the boat is pointing directly into the wind, are "luffing"
(shaking). To "fill" the sails, you will have to place the boat at an angle
to the wind. Usually this angle is 45° or more and when the boat reaches
this position the sails will fill with wind and the boat will start moving
forward. Until that point, the sails have to be manually forced out against
the wind to fill them. This is called "backing" the sail. If you want to turn
the bow of the boat to starboard (to the right) you hold the jib out to
port as in Figure 10A. The wind hits the port side of the jib and pushes
the bow to starboard. After the boat is pushed 45° to the wind, the jib is
released and trimmed normally on the starboard side.

Though backing the jib is the fastest and surest method of falling off onto
the desired tack, there are other ways. If the boat is drifting backwards as
in Figure 10B, put the tiller to starboard. The rudder will turn the stern of
the boat in the direction of the arrow and the boat will "fall off" onto the
port tack.

You might be sailing a small boat that has no jib. In that case you can
push the main out against the wind. This starts the boat moving backwards
and turns the stern to the opposite to the side that you are holding the
main. In other words, if you back the main to the starboard side, the stern
will go to port as in Figure 10C. Help the boat turn by putting the tiller to
starboard as described above.

If you are sailing a yawl or a ketch you can back the mizzen out against
the wind in the same manner and with the same effect as backing the main
of a small boat. Note Figure 10D.

The standard procedure when leaving a mooring is for a crew member to
untie the mooring line, but hold onto the end of it (or, if possible, pull the
boat forward with it to gain a little forward momentum) while he backs
the jib. When the bow is definitely swinging in the desired direction he
releases the mooring line and is off sailing!

As the boat starts moving forward, the rudder becomes effective. Though it
eventually becomes automatic, at first one has to think which way to push
the tiller to steer a sailboat. As the boat sails along, water flows past the
rudder. When the rudder is turned it deflects the water flow and pushes the
stern opposite from the direction of the deflected flow.

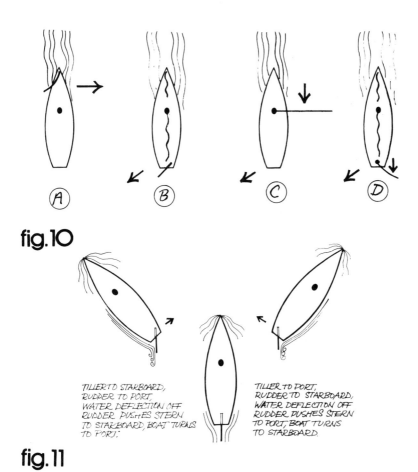

fig. 10

TILLER TO STARBOARD, RUDDER TO PORT, WATER DEFLECTION OFF RUDDER PUSHES STERN TO STARBOARD, BOAT TURNS TO PORT.

TILLER TO PORT, RUDDER TO STARBOARD, WATER DEFLECTION OFF RUDDER PUSHES STERN TO PORT, BOAT TURNS TO STARBOARD.

fig. 11

Study Figure 11. The hull and keel of the boat act as a pivotal point, so the bow goes opposite the stern. When leaving a float in a cruising boat under power, one often sees the new owner try to swing the bow out too sharply. The stern bumps along the pilings because the skipper is so intent on turning the bow he forgets he is actually throwing the stern towards the dock. To turn to port he has to push the tiller to starboard and vice-versa which confuses many beginners. It's interesting to note that the fireman who steers the rear wheels of a hook and ladder truck is called the "tillerman". The theory is the same. There's no easy way to remember how to steer a sailboat, practice is the key. Just sail on a "beam reach" (see Figures 12 and 13) and make a series of small turns to get the feel of it.

POINTS OF SAILING

Finding the Direction of the Wind

Sailing is much like riding a bicycle. When you finally catch on, you never lose the knack. Just as balance is the most important skill in bicycling, feeling the relationship of the wind to the sails is the key to sailing. Since it is impossible to actually see the wind, it usually takes quite a while for the beginner to reliably figure out where it's coming from, especially in "light air." When asked to point towards the wind a novice often points as much as $90°$ away from the true wind direction. And even should he point it out fairly well the first time, after he has turned the boat in a different direction the novice often isn't aware of the relative wind direction change since he's still facing the bow of the boat. Thus, if he pointed $50°$ off the bow the first time, he's apt to point in the same direction the second time even though the boat has changed heading.

The difficulty arises from the fact that all diagrams describing "points of sailing" (as those that follow) show the wind as nice clear black lines. The points of sailing describe the boat when sailing at various angles to the wind direction. The novice who understands fully well from books or the classroom just what is a "beat," a "reach" or a "run" is sometimes hard-pressed out on the water to relate the boat's heading to the wind direction, because the wind is not visible as in diagrams.

The way we solve this little enigma for the novice is to have him point at the wind before any maneuver, at least the first time out. We won't let him make any move until he spots the wind correctly. The easiest source of this information are "telltales," pieces of wool tied to the shrouds, which indicate wind direction.

> A note here for the racing skipper: "Angora" wool is the lightest and most sensitive, and red is the most visible. Strips of ribbon or nylon stockings are not anywhere near as sensitive and feathers are next to useless.

23

Another source is the "masthead fly" -- a swiveling weather vane at the top of the mast. This should be extremely light for three reasons. The first is the undesirability of weight near the top of the mast which causes heeling and pitching. The second is to make it sensitive to very light breezes. And the third is to reduce the moment of inertia of the masthead fly. In other words, you want it to turn to the new wind direction and settle down quickly rather than swing past it due to inertia. There are other indications of wind direction, but if the beginner sticks to telltales and the masthead fly, he can't go wrong.

In describing the direction of the wind with respect to the sails, we refer to a "tack." A boat is *always* "on a tack" unless in the process of changing tacks. Most people remember that if the wind is coming over the port side of the boat, she is on the port tack. This is fine until the boat is sailing directly downwind and the wind is coming over the stern. What tack is it on then? If you remember that legally a boat is on the tack corresponding to the opposite side her main boom is on, you can't go wrong. If the mainsail is on the starboard side of the boat, the boat is on the port tack and vice-versa. When the boat is "closehauled" (Figures 12 and 16), however, the boom is near the middle of the boat and it may be difficult for the beginner to determine which side it's on. Imagine which side it will be on if eased.

If the above methods are still confusing, there is a third way of determining tacks. If the wind is filling the port side of the mainsail, the boat is on a port tack.

Don't be confused by the three different uses of the word "tack." First, the forward lower corner of a sail is called the tack. Second, as mentioned before, a sailboat is always on the starboard or port tack, depending which side the wind is blowing. And third, a boat that is changing from one tack to the other is "tacking." There's a simple, logical reason for this apparent confusion. In the days of square-rigged ships, the forward lower corner of the squaresail on the windward side was called the tack. If the wind was coming over the port side of the ship, the port half of the squaresail was farthest forward, so the port lower corner became the tack, and the ship was on the port tack. When the ship changed course so the wind came over the starboard side, the squaresails were pivoted around so the starboard half of the sail was forward and the lower starboard corner became the tack, thus the ship has changed tacks or tacked and was now on the starboard tack.

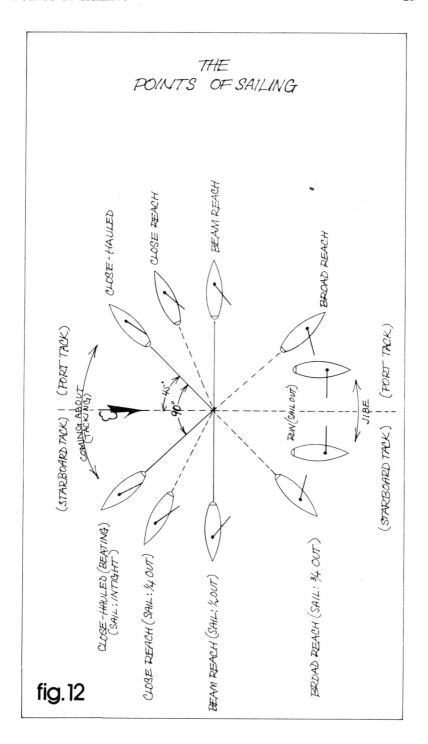

fig. 12

Reaching

The first and easiest point of sailing for the novice to practice is the "beam reach."

If he points at the wind and then turns the boat so that the wind is coming over the side of the boat at right angles to the pointing, he is sailing on a beam reach as in the diagram. This is a pleasant and forgiving point of sailing in that the boat doesn't heel (lean over) excessively and the helmsman can wander off course without accidently tacking or jibing. So a beam reach is a good heading for the beginner to get used to steering a boat.

After a little practice at steering, settle down on the beam reach with the wool telltales streaming right across the boat. Point your arm at the wind and turn the boat slightly towards the direction you're pointing. You are now sailing on a "close reach," in other words, closer to the wind than before. Your sails will start to flutter (luff), so you will have to pull them in to keep them full of wind. Picture the sail like a flag waving in the breeze. If you grab the tail of the flag and pull it towards the wind (crosswind) it will fill with air and stop flapping. This is like trimming (pulling in) the sail. As you let the flag go slowly (like easing a sail) it will start to flutter where it lines up with the wind. So, as you sail along on a reach, the test to determine whether your sail is trimmed properly is to ease it until it starts to luff at the leading edge, (miraculously) called the "luff" of of the sail and then trim it back in a little until the luff stops.

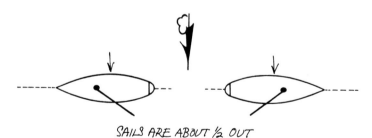

fig. 13

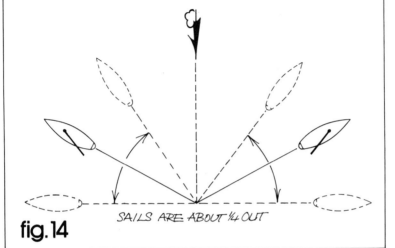

CLOSE REACHING

ANY HEADING BETWEEN CLOSE-HAULED
AND A BEAM REACH: (WIND SLIGHTLY FORWARD
OF ABEAM),

SAILS ARE ABOUT ¼ OUT

fig. 14

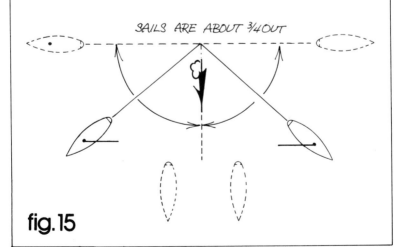

BROAD REACHING

ANY HEADING BETWEEN A BEAM REACH
AND A RUN: (WIND IS AFT OF ABEAM),

SAILS ARE ABOUT ¾ OUT

fig. 15

Sailing Closehauled

If you continue turning the boat in the direction you are pointing your arm, you will have to continue trimming in the sails to keep them from luffing. There will come a time when you can't trim in the sails any tighter, because they're almost in the middle of the boat. At this point you are sailing "closehauled" or as close to the wind as possible without actually luffing.

CLOSEHAULED

(AS CLOSE TO WIND DIRECTION AS YOUR BOAT CAN SAIL)

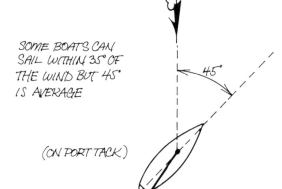

SOME BOATS CAN
SAIL WITHIN 35° OF
THE WIND BUT 45°
IS AVERAGE

45°

(ON PORT TACK)

CONTINUALLY TEST YOUR COURSE BY "PINCHING"
SLIGHTLY UNTIL THE JIB "LUFFS" AND THEN
CORRECTING TO MAKE THE JIB LUFF FIRM.

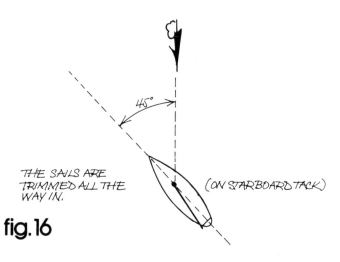

45°

THE SAILS ARE
TRIMMED ALL THE
WAY IN.

(ON STARBOARD TACK)

fig. 16

Since the sails are trimmed as tight as possible the crew can do nothing about it if the sails start luffing. The helmsman has to head more away from the wind to get the sails full again if this happens. When closehauled, it is up to the helmsman to keep the sails full. When on a reach the responsibility transfers to the crew to keep the sails full by adjusting them in or out while the helmsman steers a straight course.

Any change of course away from the wind is called "heading down" or "falling off" and any change towards the wind is "coming up" or "hardening up."

Sailors use many terms, but those that have the connotation of up or high imply being too close to the wind. Down or low imply being too far from the wind or more broadside to it. If someone says, "You're too high," he means that you are too close to the wind and your sails are either luffing slightly or about to.

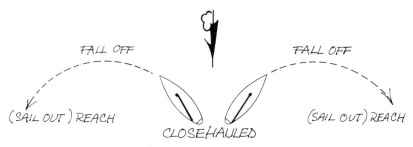

fig. 17

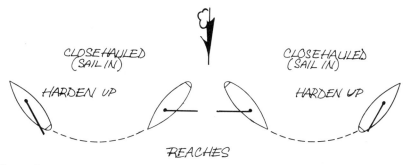

fig. 18

When sailing closehauled most boats head within 45 degrees of the wind, though some can "point" even higher (sail closer to the wind). One question often asked is how can one know the exact number of degrees your boat will sail relative to the wind. The compass gives the answer. Sail on the port tack closehauled as close to the wind as possible without luffing and record your heading. Let's say it's due north. Now sail the starboard tack closehauled and again look at your compass. The difference will likely be about 90 degrees, the compass will read due west. We assume that the wind splits right down the middle of the two tacks. Dividing the number of degrees (90°) in half, we assume you are sailing 45 degrees from the wind when closehauled. If the two headings were 80 degrees apart, it means your boat is able to sail within 40 degrees of the wind. Some boats can sail as close as 30 to 35 degrees to the wind, but this is very unusual. For our purposes we will use 45 degrees as a rule of thumb.

Running

We've covered two points of sailing -- closehauled and a reach. The third is a "run" or "running free" and is essentially sailing with the wind pushing the boat from behind. Notice in Figure 12 that the closehauled and reaching sails are at much the same angle to the wind no matter what point of sailing. As we fall off to a run, we ease the sails out to maintain this angle. We reach a point, however, seen in Figure 19, when we can't ease the sail out any further because the boom has reached the shrouds that hold up the mast. We may want to turn further, so the solution is to bring the boom over to the other side of the boat.

Whenever the boom crosses the centerline of the boat (an imaginary line from the bow to the middle of the stern) you have changed tacks. Any change of tacks (from port tack to starboard tack or vice-versa) downwind -- with the bow turning away from the source of the wind and the wind coming over the stern -- is called a "jibe." Remember the necessary ingredient is *changing tacks*. Just changing course downwind is not jibing. Until the boom crosses the centerline, you are just "falling off."

There are two commands when jibing. When the skipper issues the command, "Prepare to jibe!" the crew's job is to start trimming (pulling in) the mainsheet, so the boom won't have so far to travel when it starts swinging across.

Once the wind starts to fill the other side of the mainsail, the boom swings across the boat with fury and woe to the head that gets in its path. By trimming it in first, the crew keeps the swing of the boom to a minimum. When the helmsman sees that the boom is near the middle of the boat he gives the command of execution, "Jibe Ho!" and turns the boat. As soon as the boom crosses the centerline of the boat, the crew eases it out quickly on the other side to keep the boat from heeling excessively. This process varies with different types of boats. Many throw the boom over to the other side rather than trimming in, but this is not a safe way for the beginner to jibe until he knows his capabilities and more about the boat.

Beginners often get the boat on a run with the boom way out over the side of the boat and, after saying "Jibe Ho!" turn the boat the wrong way. If you just remember to turn the bow of the boat towards the same side of the boat as the boom, you won't make that mistake.

Because of the distance the boom has to travel across the boat when jibing, a major concern is an accidental jibe when the boom comes swinging across unexpectedly. This can happen when the wind comes over the same side of the boat as the main boom. Consider the following diagrams.

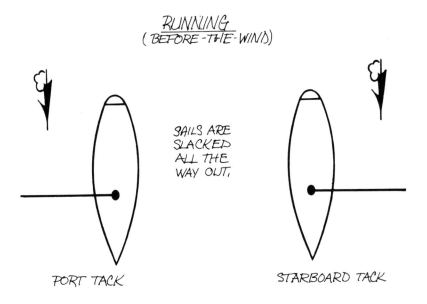

fig. 19

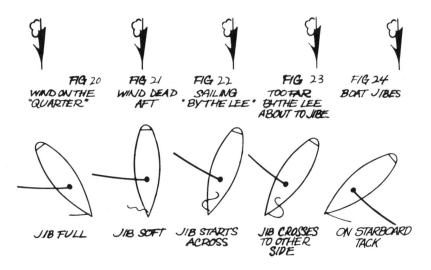

FIG 20   FIG 21   FIG 22   FIG 23   FIG 24
WIND ON THE   WIND DEAD   SAILING   TOO FAR   BOAT JIBES
"QUARTER"   AFT   "BY THE LEE"   BY THE LEE
                                ABOUT TO JIBE

JIB FULL   JIB SOFT   JIB STARTS   JIB CROSSES   ON STARBOARD
                  ACROSS   TO OTHER   TACK
                                SIDE

In Figure 20 the wind is opposite the boom, thus no fear of an accidental jibe. The jib is full.

In Figure 21 the boat is sailing dead (directly) downwind and is in no danger of jibing unless the helmsman is sloppy in his steering or a wave throws the stern to one side. The jib is being blanketed by the main (no wind is getting to it).

Figure 22 shows the wind on the same side as the boom. Though dangerous, a boat can sail along like this. It's called sailing "by-the-lee." The wind is coming over the "leeward" side of the boat. You might think this would make it the windward side because the wind is now hitting that side first, but right of way rules, to avoid confusion, define the "leeward side" as the side over which the main boom is carried.

If you sail too far by-the-lee as in Figure 23, the wind will catch the other side of the sail and throw it across the boat. The boom will raise up in the air, unless held down by a "boom vang," and can catch on the backstay if the latter is close to the end of the boom as in some boats. The accidental jibe is often called a "flying jibe" and if the boom catches on the backstay, it's called a "goosewing." The first warning of an accidental jibe is the jib coming across the boat. When the jib crosses to the other side, the main won't be far behind so WATCH OUT!

One of my favorite friends is a grand lady who sails Atlantic Class sailboats which are 30-foot sloops of identical design. She is over 80 years old and still racing, almost always with an all-girl crew and often with someone who has never sailed before. She told me the following incident happened when she was in her 70's. One of her crew had never sailed before, and so was assigned the job of trimming in the mainsail for the jibe around a mark while the rest of her crew, who were more experienced, took care of more difficult tasks.

Beforehand the skipper carefully described the job: "Trim the mainsail with the mainsheet, but don't make it fast." In other words, pull in the line that adjusts the sail in and out but don't cleat or secure it. Just before the mark she gave the command, "Prepare to jibe!" at which time the new crew member started pulling in the mainsheet hand over hand at a snail's pace. Terribly agitated because they were barreling down on the mark with boats at close quarters all around them, our lady skipper cried to "hurry it up" to which she received an extremely haughty, "But you said, don't make it fast!"

This is an example of the reason we are covering all the various terms which may seem confusing at first. PROPER COMMUNICATION ON A BOAT IS AN ABSOLUTE NECESSITY OR ACCIDENTS CAN RESULT.

Having jibed, as in Figure 24, we can steer any course on the starboard tack all the way up to "closehauled" just by "hardening up" and this is a good exercise in learning the feel of different points of sail.

Beating

Now, imagine we want to reach a destination that is directly upwind of us. We know by now that we can't sail closer to the wind than 45 degrees so we must zig-zag first on one tack and then on the other until we reach it. Each turn we make from port to starboard and vice-versa with the bow pointing momentarily into the wind is called a "tack", "tacking" or "coming about." A series of tacks is called a "beat" or "beating to windward."

The command of preparation for a tack is: "Stand by to come about," or, more usually, "Ready about!" Upon hearing this the crew's main job is to get the jib ready for the tack by uncleating, but not releasing it, and preparing to take in on the opposite jib sheet. The main, which is near the middle of the boat when closehauled, is of no concern because it has only a short distance to travel and the breeze carries it across automatically. The crew should say "Ready," then the skipper puts the helm (the tiller or steering wheel) over and gives the command of execution "Hard Alee!" at the same time. The latter term is an Americanization of the command "Helm's Alee!" which means the helm is put to the leeward side of the boat. The "windward" of anything is that which wind strikes first, while the "leeward" (usually pronounced "looward" is that which the wind strikes next.

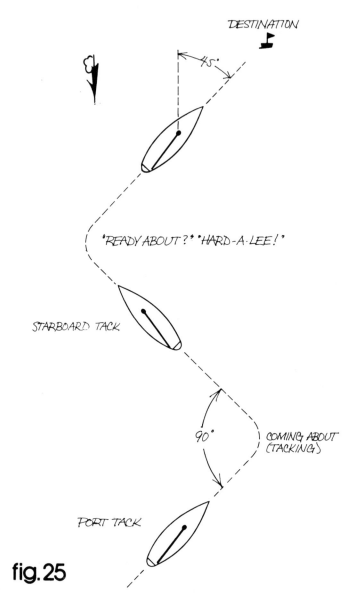

fig. 25

If a beachball were being propelled by the wind across the water, the side of the boat it hits first is the windward side. Thus, the other side is the leeward side. Of two boats, the boat it hits first is the windward boat and next the leeward boat. The same holds true for windward or leeward islands, marks, or whatever object you are referring to. For instance, two boats may be approaching on a collision course, one closehauled beating to windward and the other running free. The wind is hitting the boat running downwind first so it is the "windward boat" and since it is hitting the boat beating upwind next, it is called the "leeward boat." This can seem wrong even to sailors who have a reasonable amount of experience, but is important to remember for reasons of right-of-way which will be explained later.

Returning to "tacking," whenever the tiller is put to leeward the boat turns towards the wind. When you point to the wind and turn the bow in that direction, you are tacking (when you actually change tacks). Remember the two "T's" -- *T*ack *T*owards the wind.

Sometimes the boat fails to complete a tack (or "come about") and ends up dead in the water head to wind. In other words, the bow is pointed into the wind and the boat is motionless. Without motion or "way on" there is no water flowing past the rudder. As mentioned before when discussing leaving a mooring, the rudder has to deflect water in order to turn the boat, so the "wayless" boat has no "steerageway." Turning the rudder doesn't turn the boat. A boat in this predicament is said, as explained on pages 19 and 20, to be "in irons."

Usually this happens to the inexperienced helmsman who allows the boat to slow up too much before attempting to tack. Then a wave stops the boat in the middle of the tack leaving the boat in irons. It is a temporary condition since the boat will shortly fall off to one tack or the other. The only problem is that it may not be the desired tack. If, for instance, the reason for the tack was a moored boat dead ahead, it could be very embarrassing (and costly) to get in irons and then fall back on the same tack. The boat doesn't gain steerageway until it gains speed, so by the time you speed up enough to try to tack again, you may collide with the moored boat.

The helmsman often isn't totally at fault when a boat ends up in irons. If the mainsail remains cleated during a tack and the crew doesn't get the jib trimmed in on the new tack fast enough, the main may force the boat up into the wind again. By this time the boat has lost so much, forward momentum that she is in irons.

The main does not need to be uncleated when tacking, but it is a good idea for the skipper to hold the mainsheet at all times when sailing amongst moored boats. If a gust of wind hits the boat the alert skipper can release the mainsheet which spills the wind out of the main and lets the boat straighten up. In a centerboard boat this can avert a capsize.

The other way to reduce the force of the wind on the sails (which causes the boat to heel way over) is to head more into the wind and thereby luff the sails. In small doses this is called "feathering" the boat to windward, but in response to a strong gust it is simply luffing.

Circle of Courses

The foregoing has been a description of the various points of sailing. Actually whenever we turn a boat substantially we change from one point of sailing to another. If we turned the boat in a tight 360 degrees, its wake would describe a circle and we would have passed through all the points of sailing, however briefly. It is sometimes easier for the beginner to think of the boat always being on one part of the circle as in Figure 26.

As you can see in the diagrams, whenever the boat turns its sail trim will correspond to one of the positions on the "circle of courses" diagram.

You can get your boat from any course (port or starboard tack) aimed towards any specific destination by making a circle in either direction (clockwise or counterclockwise, except that you must tack your way directly upwind). Just begin by pointing the boat in the direction that is closest to the destination and make the necessary sail adjustments. When a "come about" or a "jibe" is involved there is usually a shortest way. (See Figures 28 and 29.)

Collision Avoidance

There is one matter of great importance before you go out sailing the first time: Collision avoidance. Though we will go into right-of-way rules later, it is the responsibility of the helmsman to avoid a collision. He must be constantly on the lookout for potential trouble and, though he can delegate a crew member to help keep an eye out, the ultimate responsibility is his. This means that if the boat is heeling and the sails block his view to leeward, he must occasionally peek under the boom. If another boat is heading your way there is one sure way of determining whether or not it's on a collision course. Note the bearing of the boat either by using the compass or by lining it up with some item on your boat such as a lifeline, stanchion or a shroud. If, in a short time, you take the bearing again and it hasn't changed, you are on a collision course as in Figure 30. Relative speeds of the two boats make no difference at all. You could be sailing at five knots and be on a collision course with a ship traveling at 25 knots, if the bearing doesn't change.

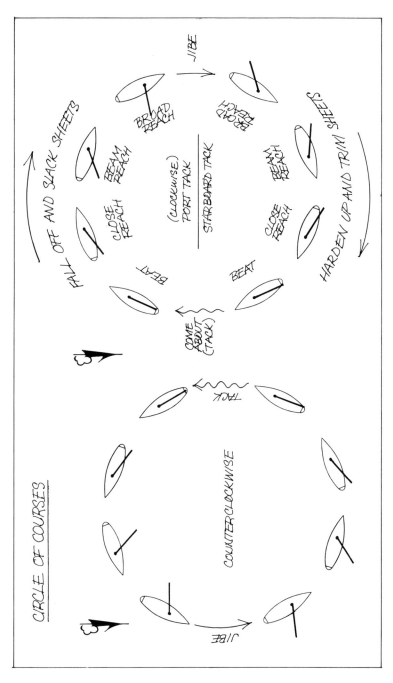

fig. 26

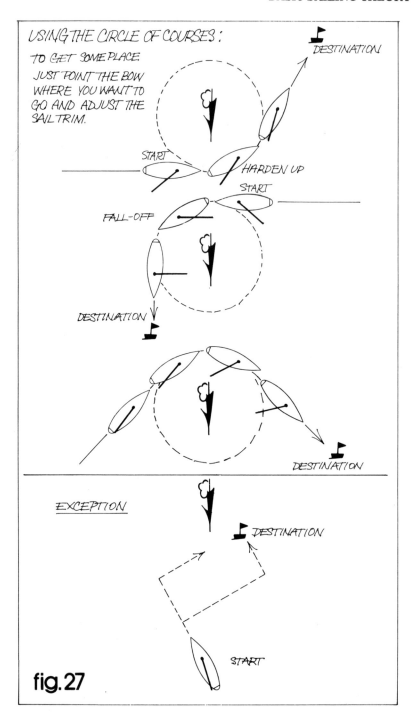

USING THE CIRCLE OF COURSES :

TO GET SOME PLACE
JUST POINT THE BOW
WHERE YOU WANT TO
GO AND ADJUST THE
SAIL TRIM.

DESTINATION

START

HARDEN UP

START

FALL-OFF

DESTINATION

DESTINATION

EXCEPTION

DESTINATION

START

fig. 27

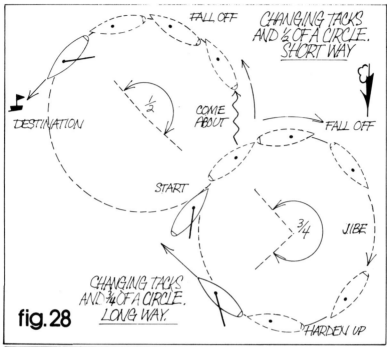

fig. 28

CHANGING TACKS AND ½ OF A CIRCLE. _SHORT WAY_

CHANGING TACKS AND ¾ OF A CIRCLE. _LONG WAY._

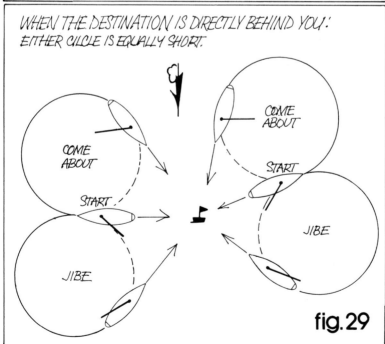

WHEN THE DESTINATION IS DIRECTLY BEHIND YOU: EITHER CIRCLE IS EQUALLY SHORT.

fig. 29

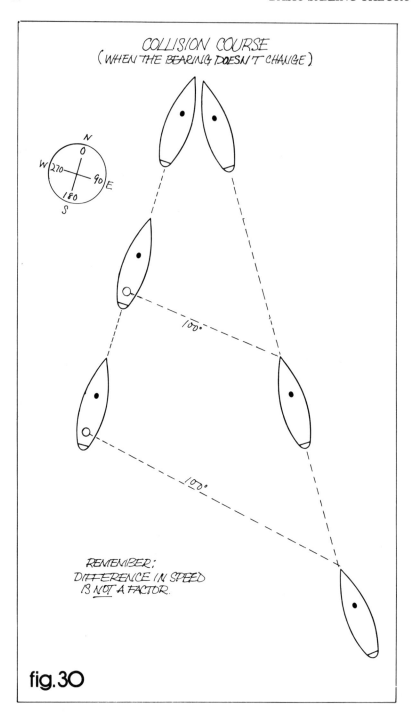

fig.30

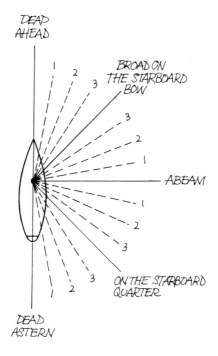

fig.31

If a crew member spots a boat that may be a potential hazard, he must point it out quickly to the skipper in terms that describe its location accurately. The words in Figure 31 are those the crew member would say to indicate a hazard at the various positions.

If you want to pinpoint the location further, you describe the hazard in "points." There are 32 points in the 360 degrees of a compass (11¼ degrees for each point). The dotted lines indicate the points (eight to a quadrant). Starting from abeam, you have "1, 2 or 3 points forward of abeam" and "1, 2 or 3 points abaft abeam" (aft of abeam). There are "1, 2 or 3 points on the starboard bow" and "1, 2 or 3 points on the starboard quarter." This covers one side of the boat. The other side is exactly the same, but with "port" substituted for "starboard."

Additional Knots

The last subject covered in the first class are knots. Two have already been covered -- the "figure-eight" and the "stop" knot. One of the most useful knots you can know for sailing is the "bowline" which is pronounced "bōlin." It is used to make a non-slip loop for towing, docking, and a multitude of other purposes. Its major attribute is that no matter how

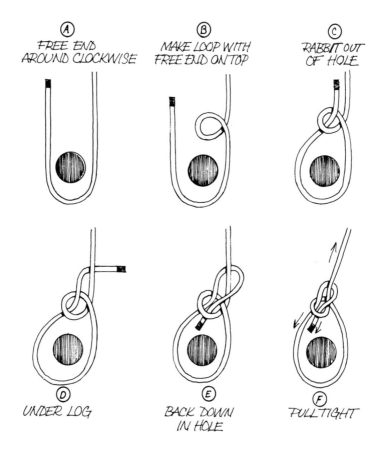

fig. 32

much strain is put on the knot, it can be easily untied (unlike some knots that tighten up when strain is applied). Though there are many ways of teaching people how to tie it, the time-honored one has a rabbit coming out of his hole (the loop), running under a log (the standing part of the line), and going back down the hole. The object is to get the end of the line back through the loop the same way it came out. When you can tie this one in the pitch dark, on a heaving deck, with one hand, you're an old salt!

TEST QUESTIONS -- SECTION ONE

1. What is LOA?
2. What is LWL?
3. Where is beam measured?
4. What are topsides?
5. What is aspect ratio?
6. What is ballast-displacement ratio?
7. What is the difference between a ketch and a yawl?
8. Define a cutter.
9. Does a schooner have a mizzen?
10. What is the difference between standing and running rigging?
11. What is the difference between stays and shrouds?
12. What is the difference between halyards and sheets?
13. What are the names of the three corners of a sail?
14. What are the edge areas between the corners called?
15. What is the extra material in a convex sail called?
16. What is freeboard?
17. What corner of the jib is attached first?
18. Name three ways of recognizing the above corner?
19. Which sail do you raise first?
20. Describe a boat that is in irons.
21. What are telltales?
22. What are the commands when tacking? Jibing?
23. What is the location of the main boom on a starboard tack run?
24. What is a beat?
25. What is luffing?
26. What is hardening up?
27. What is by-the-lee?
28. What is leeward?
29. Why should you be ready to release the mainsheet in a hurry on a centerboard boat?
30. How do you know if you're on a collision course?
31. If a crew told you there was a boat on your starboard quarter, where would you look?

SAILS AND WIND

In recent years a great deal has been learned about the relationship between wind and sails. For a long time people thought the wind just pushed the sails. Even though this force was sideways when closehauled, the wedge shape of the keel was supposed to squirt the boat forward. Though not entirely accurate, the theory isn't too far off. The wind exerts both a sideways force and a forward pull on the sail. In simplest terms, the keel keeps the boat from slipping sideways, so all that is left is the forward pull.

The forward pull is caused by air flowing over the surface of the sail as it does over an airplane wing. Air splits as it passes on either side of an

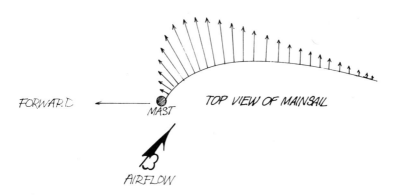

FORWARD ← MAST · TOP VIEW OF MAINSAIL

AIRFLOW

fig.33

airplane wing. Because of the curvature of the upper surface of the wing, the air passing over that side has to travel a greater distance than that passing under the wing. Since it has to go farther, it has to go faster in order to reach the trailing edge at the same time as the air flowing past the underside of the wing. Daniel Bernoulli discovered in 1738 that this increased velocity meant a corresponding decrease in atmospheric pressure, i.e., suction. This suction acts at right angles to the surface and the amount of suction can be diagrammed as in Figure 33. The longest arrows represent the greatest suction. The higher the velocity on both sides, the greater the suction; and the greater the difference in velocity between the sides, the greater the suction.

The air has to flow over the surface smoothly and evenly, though. Once the air starts to "separate" from the surface it becomes turbulent. Instead of an even flow, burbles develop that reduce suction. Much of the turbulence is caused by the angle that the airfoil makes with the airflow. This is called the "angle of attack" or "angle of incidence." If the angle is small as pictured in Figure 34A the airflow remains "attached" to the surface for quite a distance back towards the leech of the sail or the trailing edge of a wing. When the angle is increased as in Figure 34B, the

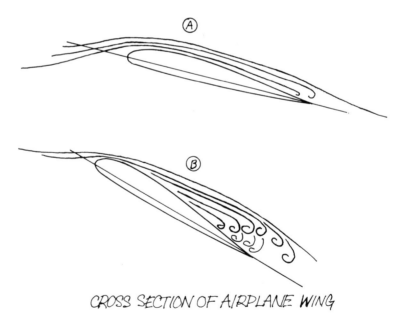

CROSS SECTION OF AIRPLANE WING

fig.34

airflow detaches earlier and turbulence works its way forward. At a certain angle and speed there is so much separation of flow that the wing no longer develops enough suction or "lift" and a stall occurs. In an airplane the result is dramatic since the aircraft will drop suddenly. A sailboat, however, will just heel over more and slow down.

Up to the stall point, however, the greater the angle of attack the greater the lift derived. Imagine the wing in Figure 34A as symmetrical, instead of asymmetrical. All other lifting surfaces of a yacht are symmetrical -- the keel, hull, centerboard and rudder. Yet they can still develop lift because of the angle the water hits them, the angle of attack, as we will see later in the chapter on Hull and Sails. In the diagram, the air hitting the underside of the wing travels a lesser distance than that which has to travel around the leading edge and over the top, so suction develops. In addition, the deflection of the air or water is like the lift a child's hand gets when he sticks it out of a car window and tilts it upward.

A man told me one time that he and his friends, newly introduced to the sport of sailing, decided to forego all nautical lingo in favor of flying terms. He claimed they were much more descriptive. For instance, he said when the sail luffed they would say, "Pull it in, it's stalling."

As we can see from the foregoing, they had their terms backwards. The sail stalls if it is trimmed in too tight. If a sail is eased to the point just before it luffs, we can be certain it isn't stalled and is properly trimmed. A luff is easy to see because the leading edge of the sail is flapping. *A stalled sail, however, looks the same as one operating at maximum efficiency.*

So that's the reason for the basic rule of sail trimming: EASE THE SAIL UN-TIL IT LUFFS AND THEN TRIM IT IN JUST ENOUGH TO STOP THE LUFF. This is a good rule for beginners, but after you have sailed for a while you may find, especially on reaches, the need to trim in a little past this point to get maximum drive from the sail. The judgement depends a great deal on wind strength. In lighter winds you can trim in tighter before separation and turbulence occurs. Of course, the tighter you trim in, the more sideways is the driving force. So although greater than before, it may be transmitted more into detrimental heeling than into beneficial forward driving force.

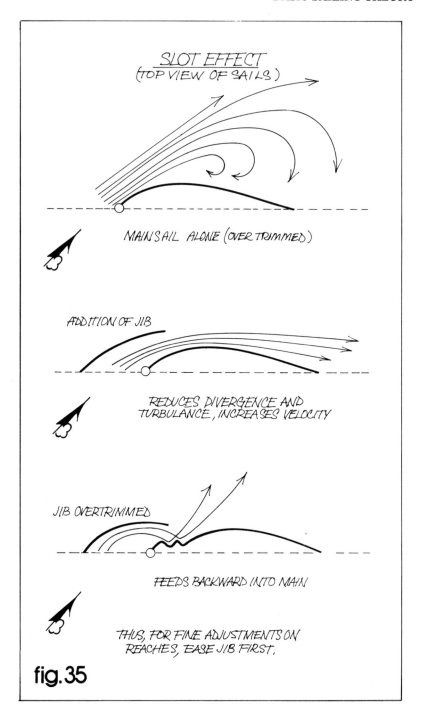

SLOT EFFECT
(TOP VIEW OF SAILS)

MAINSAIL ALONE (OVER TRIMMED)

ADDITION OF JIB

REDUCES DIVERGENCE AND
TURBULANCE, INCREASES VELOCITY

JIB OVERTRIMMED

FEEDS BACKWARD INTO MAIN

THUS, FOR FINE ADJUSTMENTS ON
REACHES, EASE JIB FIRST,

fig.35

Slot Effect

Boats with jibs have added advantages over those without. First, the jib is a very efficient sail since there is no mast in front of it to disrupt the airflow. Second, it bends and funnels the air behind the main. The funneling action tends to increase the speed of the air flowing past the leeward side of the main. This, because of Bernoulli's Principle, increases the suction and efficiency of the main. As we have mentioned before, the faster the air travels, the less it can bend around the sail curvature. Luckily, the jib not only speeds up the air, but bends it aft so it can follow the main curvature more easily. This velocity increase and bending is called "slot effect," the "slot" being the opening between the main and the jib. The result is that though a boat can sail under just mainsail or just the jib, the combination of main *and* jib add up to greater effectiveness than the sum of each alone.

Heeling

For many reasons, some of which will be covered later, "heeling" is an enemy to the sailor. If a boat is closehauled, the sail trimmed in tight, many of the force arrows point sideways, as in Figure 36A. In other words, there is a large sideways push resulting in the boat heeling (leaning over). As the sail is eased out for a reach (Figure 36B) the arrows start to line up more with the course of the boat. The result is less heeling and more forward pull. A reach, therefore, is usually the fastest point of sailing.

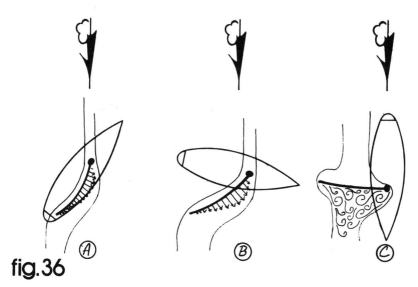

fig.36   (A)   (B)   (C)

It may appear that you're sailing faster when closehauled, because there's a great deal of commotion. The boat is heeling over, plowing through the seas, and the wind seems stronger because you're moving towards it. When you fall off to a reach, the commotion quiets down. You're sailing across the wind and the sea and neither seems as powerful. The boat is more upright because the pull of the sails is more forward. Carrying this one step further, you might think that a run would be even faster because the wind and the boat are both going in the same direction. On a run, though, the wind can't flow over both sides of the sail which is necessary for any suction to develop on the leeward side of the sail. So the wind is just pushing the boat. As you can see in Figure 36C there is pure turbulence behind the sail downwind. Were a jib present it would be "blanketed" by the main; i.e., no wind would be reaching it because of the main being in between it and the wind.

When the wind velocity increases to the point where a given boat on a reach is "overpowered," heeling excessively in comparison to forward drive, a faster point of sailing would then be a run.

Wind Shifts

For the highest efficiency, sails must be adjusted so they make just the proper angle to the wind. Since the wind is constantly changing direction, this means the sails must be constantly adjusted to the various shifts.

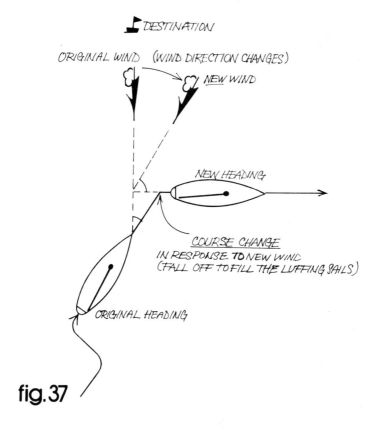

A HEADER: WIND SHIFTS FORWARD ON THE BOAT

DESTINATION

ORIGINAL WIND   (WIND DIRECTION CHANGES)

NEW WIND

NEW HEADING

COURSE CHANGE
IN RESPONSE TO NEW WIND
(FALL OFF TO FILL THE LUFFING SAILS)

ORIGINAL HEADING

fig.37

A shift of the "true" wind direction, the actual wind, is called either a "header" or a "lift" depending on the relationship of the shift to the heading of the boat. Figure 37 shows a boat closehauled on the port tack. If the wind shifts more towards the bow of the boat, causing the sails to luff, necessitating a change of course away from the wind to keep them filled, the boat has been "headed" or has "sailed into a header."

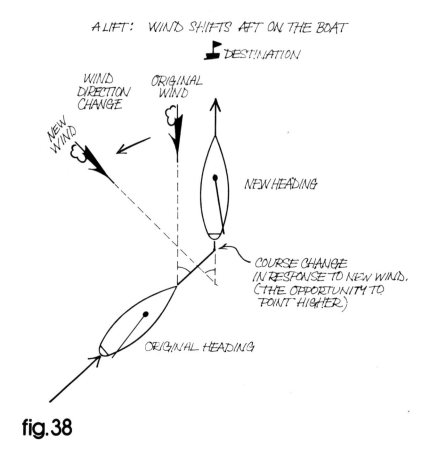

fig. 38

If the wind shifts more towards the stern of the boat, allowing the skipper to steer higher than before, he has been "lifted" or is sailing "in a lift."

A header or a lift occurring on a reach means a corresponding sail adjustment -- trimming for a header and easing for a lift -- while maintaining a constant heading.

A wind shift that is a header for a boat on a port tack is a lift for a boat on the starboard tack. The boat sailing on a lift will reach his desired

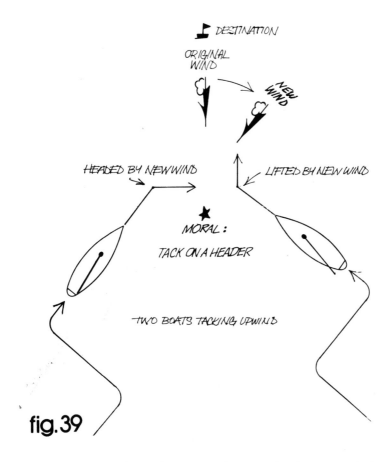

DESTINATION

ORIGINAL WIND

NEW WIND

HEADED BY NEW WIND

LIFTED BY NEW WIND

★
MORAL:

TACK ON A HEADER

TWO BOATS TACKING UPWIND

fig.39

upwind destination faster than one sailing in a header. A standard sailboat racing axiom, therefore, is "if you're headed, tack."

When a wind shift is described in relation to a compass direction, it is said to be "veering" or "backing." A veering wind is one that is shifting clockwise.

For instance, a wind that shifts from north to northeast is "veering." A shift from east to northeast is "backing" in that the shift is counterclockwise. A north wind is one that blows from the north. Don't confuse this with *current* which is named for the direction *to* which it flows. A northerly current is one that flows from the south.

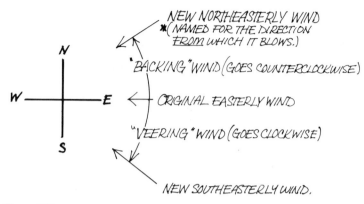

fig.40

The foregoing shifts are changes in the direction of the actual wind blowing over the water. Another type of shift, which also causes the need for sail adjustment is a change in the "apparent wind" direction.

Apparent Wind

"Apparent wind" is a very simple concept that continues to mystify many people who have been sailing for years.

It is the resultant wind derived from the wind produced by the boat moving through the air and the wind produced by nature -- the "true wind." Thus, it is the wind you feel on the boat. Cigarette smoke, telltales, electronic wind direction indicators of cruising boats all show the apparent wind direction. We often get the comment from people the first time out, "You said we sail within 45 degrees of the wind when closehauled, but the wool on the shrouds indicates we're sailing almost into the wind." This is their first experience with apparent wind on a sailboat.

Imagine yourself standing up in a convertible. It is a calm day, so there's no true wind. As the convertible starts forward, you will begin to feel a breeze on your face that increases as the speed of the car increases. At 10 mph you will feel a 10 mph breeze on your face. This is apparent wind.

Now imagine yourself in the same car heading north and there's an easterly wind of 10 mph blowing. It is hitting the right side of your face. As the car starts forward you will not feel two different winds, one on the side and one on the front of your face, but a resultant wind coming from an angle forward of the true wind.

By drawing, to a consistent scale, a parallelogram from the boat speed and the true wind, you can determine the force and direction of the apparent wind. Let's say your boat tacks in 80 degrees. That means the true wind is 40 degrees off your bow. If, for example, the boat speed is six knots and the true wind is twelve knots, measure off the units. Then draw a parallelogram, the diagonal of which is the apparent wind. By measuring the length of the diagonal, you can determine the speed in knots of the apparent wind.

In this example (see Figure 41) it is 17 knots, and bears 27 degrees from your heading versus 40 degrees for the true wind. Notice how the direction of the apparent wind changes with the true wind in the following diagrams. (For the purposes of these diagrams we'll keep true wind speed and boat speed constant, which would only be the case at different points of sailing if the boats were different sizes.)

There are four points that are obvious from these diagrams. First, the apparent wind is always forward of the true wind (unless the true wind is dead ahead or astern). Second, as the true wind comes aft, the apparent wind lessens in velocity. Third, when the true wind is well aft, a small change in true wind direction makes a large change in apparent wind direction. And fourth, when the boat is on a beam reach or closehauled, the apparent wind is of greater velocity than the true wind.

The first point is important when considering when to jibe. Since it is desirable to sail at the slight angle to the wind rather than dead downwind, you may not be heading to your desired destination and will have to jibe to reach it. It's important, therefore, to determine the direction of the true wind and the angle your heading is making with it. If you know you are steering 20 degrees from dead downwind on one tack, then you will be on the same point of sailing when you are 20 degrees from dead downwind on the other tack. The point of jibing should come when your destination bears 40 degrees off your bow from your present heading. The key, of course, is determining the direction of the true wind. By glancing at your telltales and at the wind signs on the water -- like streaks and ripples -- you can judge about how far aft of the apparent wind the true wind is.

A more positive way of determining true wind direction is by heading off momentarily until the apparent wind and the true wind line up, i.e., dead downwind. The difference between the new heading and your former heading, 20 degrees in the example above, when doubled (40°), is the number of degrees in which you'll jibe.

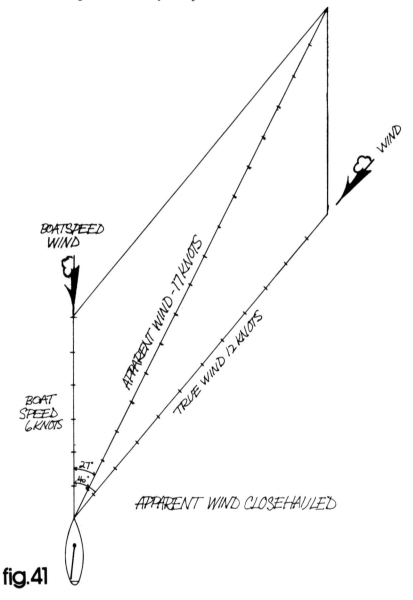

fig.41

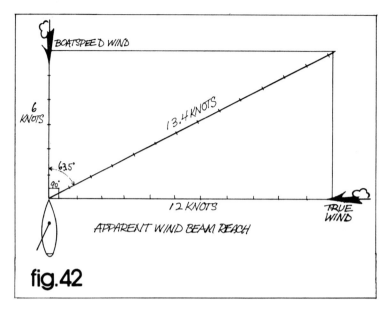

BOATSPEED WIND

6 KNOTS

13.4 KNOTS

63.5°

90°

12 KNOTS

TRUE WIND

APPARENT WIND BEAM REACH

fig.42

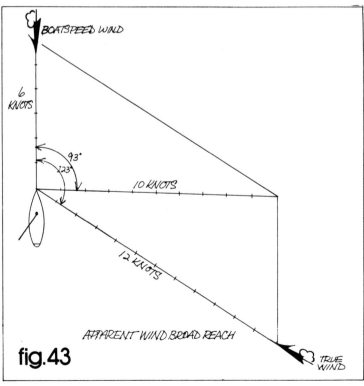

BOATSPEED WIND

6 KNOTS

93°

123°

10 KNOTS

12 KNOTS

APPARENT WIND BROAD REACH

TRUE WIND

fig.43

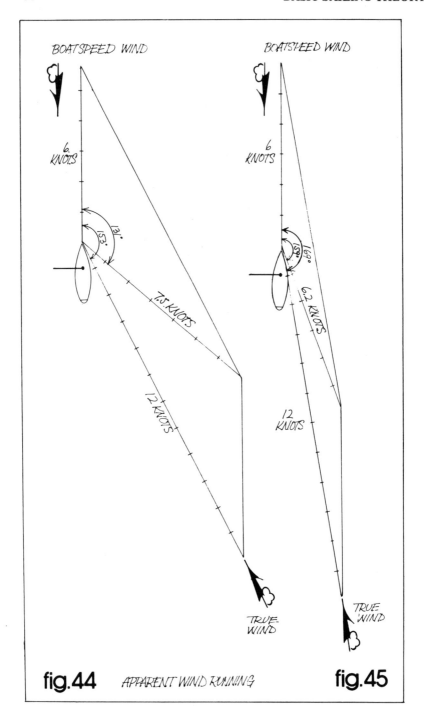

BOATSPEED WIND

BOATSPEED WIND

6. KNOTS

6 KNOTS

131°

153°

169°

153°

7.5 KNOTS

6.2 KNOTS

12 KNOTS

12 KNOTS

TRUE WIND

TRUE WIND

fig.44   *APPARENT WIND RUNNING*   **fig.45**

The second point, that as that true wind comes aft, the apparent wind speed lessens, is obvious if you have ever seen powerboats head downwind. Sometimes they cruise along at the same speed and direction as the true wind. Their exhaust hangs around the boat, an enveloping cloud (one reason we sail!), and the apparent wind is just about zero.

This lessening of the wind speed you feel on the boat and thereby the force of the wind on the sails can lull you into forgetting the difference when you round a mark and start on a beat. You may have started your sailing outing on a run, so you had no idea of the apparent wind strength on a beat. Or the wind may have increased during the run. Either way you must consider the possibility that you many have to shorten sail on a cruising boat when you come up on a beat, and it is easiest to change jibs while still on the run. Let's say a boat is going nine knots in a 16 knot breeze. If dead downwind the apparent wind is the true wind minus the boat speed, or just seven knots. This doesn't feel like much wind and the force on the sails is relatively light. When the boat starts beating she may slow down to six knots, but the apparent wind increases to almost 21 knots. You would assume that since the apparent wind is now three times greater than the downwind velocity, it exerts three times the force against the sails. Wrong. The force of the wind *quadruples* as the velocity doubles, so the wind force is *nine times greater* on the closehauled course than on the run in this case. Couple this with the increased heeling moment of the closehauled course, and the boat many very well be overpowered. You should have had the forethought during the run to shorten sail.

The third point we made about the apparent wind diagrams was that, when the true wind was well aft, a small change in true wind direction makes a large change in apparent wind direction. Compare Figure 43 with Figure 44. A 30 degree change in true wind direction made a 38 degree change in apparent wind. In comparing Figure 44 with Figure 45, we find a 16 degree change in true wind makes a 28 degree change in apparent wind. This, among other things, is what makes steering dead downwind so difficult. A small swing by the lee actually results in an exaggerated swing of the apparent wind by the lee. This can cause oscillation as the apparent wind swings madly back and forth from one side of the boat to the other on relatively minor changes in heading. At worst, it can force a flying jibe on the inexperienced helmsman.

The fourth point was that when a boat is reaching or beating, the apparent wind is of greater velocity than the true wind. You are, in effect, "making your own wind." In iceboating it is an important part of the resulting high speeds. The speed record for iceboats is over 140 mph. The wind was probably around 50 mph. So obviously it was "created" wind. The faster the boat went, the higher the wind velocity it created. Only because of the lack of friction can these high speeds be attained. A normal sailboat is limited in speed by hull resistance, skin friction and wave making drag, so it cannot take full advantage of the increased apparent wind velocity. A planing sailboat is more apt to get up on a high-speed plane on a reach than a run just because of this apparent wind increase. Even so, the faster a boat is to windward, the more closewinded (able to head close to the wind) it must be.

In the first set of wind diagrams, everything remained constant except the direction of the true wind which was moved further aft in each subsequent diagram. Now let us change the boat speed and the wind velocity keeping the true wind direction at 45 degrees off the bow.

Notice in Figure 46 that initially the wind speed was 10 knots and the boat speed four knots. The dotted extension of the true wind line indicates a four knot increase or puff. So we see a basic axiom: "In a puff the apparent wind comes aft." To be correct this necessitates a constant speed on the boat's part. Generally, however, by the time the boat picks up speed the puff has passed, so the axiom holds true.

We already know that we point higher in order to reduce heeling when hit by an overpowering gust. This axiom shows another reason to do the same thing. As the gust hits the apparent wind goes aft causing more heeling and less drive and changing the angle of incidence, the angle the apparent wind makes with the sails, so that the sails now are improperly trimmed unless you head up or ease sheets or traveler. This change in apparent wind direction is important to remember even on light days. On days when you have a three mph breeze, the wind velocity in a puff is apt to be more than double the regular breeze. When it is blowing 15 mph, gusts may get to only 20-22 mph or about a third higher. Thus, the change in apparent wind direction aft is often greater on light days than on heavy ones.

The dot-dash lines in the diagram show the resulting change in apparent wind when the wind dies suddenly. With the boat speed remaining constant and the wind velocity lowering to six knots, the apparent wind goes forward. This is one of the reasons that small catamarans rarely carry spinnakers. The hulls have very little resistance to the water, and downwind the cats sail almost as fast as the wind making it very difficult to keep a spinnaker drawing. If the wind dies for a moment, the spinnaker collapses and it is very difficult to get it filled until the boat slows down. Therefore, small cats, much like iceboats, tack downwind by jibing. By sailing from reach to reach they pick up greater speed and make up the extra distance sailed.

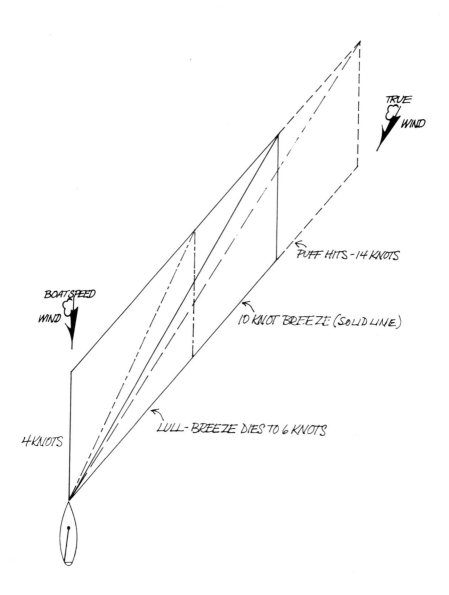

fig.46

458

458

SAIL TRIM

To sail well, we must allow for the shifts in the true and apparent wind and still maintain the optimum drive angle of the wind to the sails by both judicious helmsmanship and proper sail trim. By imagining the air flowing past the sails as smoke, one can get a much better idea of proper sail trim. Many wind tunnel tests (called "smoke visualization tests") have been done with smoke blowing past sails. The difference between smooth flow and turbulent flow is very easy to see. Obviously we can't create a smoke-screen in front of our sailboat, but we can do the next best thing: attach telltales to the sails so they indicate whether the flow past the sail is turbulent or smooth.

This has been done very successfully with jibs and has been tried on mainsails with much less success. The most practical method is to thread a needle with some light wool of a high visibility color and pass it through the sail. Cut it off leaving about five inches to hang out on either side of the sail and tie two small overhand knots right next to the sailcloth so the wool won't pull through. By using a long piece of wool, pulling it right through to five inches from the end, and cutting it off five inches from the cloth, you can repeat the process at other points on the sail without having to rethread the needle. Another good practice is to place the wool higher on one side of the sail than on the other. In certain sunlight conditions it's hard to tell which piece of wool is which unless they are at different levels. Some people place tape on either side of the sail in fear that the needle hole will weaken the material, but the edges of the tape tend to loosen and the wool hangs up on them and on its adhesive. Eventually the tape comes off anyway, so it's best not to use it in the first place.

The telltales should be placed in three positions along the luff of the jib about six to twelve inches from the leading edge depending on the size of the boat. Make sure that the wool cannot touch a seam or any sail stitching, because the hairs of the wool will catch on anything rough. A type of wool should be used that has as few tiny hairs as possible. Though Angora wool makes the best shroud telltales because of its mass to weight very light and fuzzy), it is definitely not the type to use next which the fuzz hangs up on.

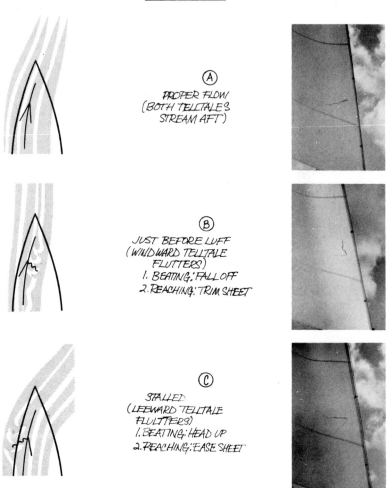

TOP VIEW OF JIB

(A)
PROPER FLOW
(BOTH TELLTALES
STREAM AFT)

(B)
JUST BEFORE LUFF
(WINDWARD TELLTALE
FLUTTERS)
1. BEATING: FALL OFF
2. REACHING: TRIM SHEET

(C)
STALLED
(LEEWARD TELLTALE
FLUTTERS)
1. BEATING: HEAD UP
2. REACHING: EASE SHEET

fig.47

Now watch the middle set of telltales on the jib as you change your heading without varying your jib trim. In Figures 47A and B, you will notice that as the boat heads up towards the wind, the windward telltales will start to flutter. Conversely, when the boat heads too far off the wind, as in Figure 47C, the leeward telltale flutters because the angle of incidence (angle of attack) becomes so great that the wind is hitting mostly on the windward side of the sail. This disrupts the flow over the lee side and turbulence results. To the sailor this is most important. If there is turbulence on the lee side, the sail, as an airfoil, is stalled and thereby does not produce the desired drive. Again, a luff is easy to see because the sail starts to flutter, but a stall isn't. We've said before that the greater the angle of attack, the greater the drive until separation begins. With the jib telltales described (plus a few others further back on the sail) we can trim the jib until the leeward telltales start to flutter. You'll find it's a very fine line between a luff and a stall, probably between a 5 to 10 degree change in heading or angle of attack.

Telltales are very helpful for the beginner and yet can be used to advantage by the expert. The sailor who is beginning to learn to sail to windward, by using these telltales, may use a very simple rule (dubbed "Reinhorn's Law" in honor of Dr. Reinhorn -- an Offshore Sailing School student of 1967). The rule reads, "Point the tiller at the fluttering piece of wool." If the leeward wool is fluttering, it's because the boat is being sailed too "hard," too far away from the wind for the desired closehauled course, and should be pointed more towards the wind. Putting the tiller to leeward cures this. If the windward piece of wool is fluttering the boat is being sailed too close to the wind, on the verge of a luff. Putting the tiller to windward causes the boat to fall off and solves the problem.

There are some top skippers who consider these telltales a crutch for incompetence, because they have learned to sail properly without them. They have a point when you are sailing closehauled and the skipper is steering entirely by wool on the jib. One of the mistakes that many skippers make is trying to keep the jib completely full without allowing the windward (or leeward) piece of wool to flutter. There are many conditions, however, when this shouldn't be done. For instance, in a strong wind and smooth sea you may be able to "pinch" (carry a very slight luff in the jib) and still maintain your speed or even go faster. If you fall off until the sail is full, excessive heeling reduces the speed of the boat. So the experienced helmsman takes the wool on the jib with a grain of salt and steers what he feels to be the fastest course for the existing conditions.

There are two conditions when the jib telltales really come into their own. The first is reaching. While racing the jib should be "played" constantly on a reach. This means a crew member must ease it when it stalls and trim it when it luffs. He should have his eyes glued to the telltales near the luff of the sail and the jib sheet in his hand whether a small boat or a Twelve Meter. Without the wool on the jib it is *very, very* difficult to determine if the sail is stalled.

As with everything else about sailing, there are exceptions. When the reach becomes very broad and approaches a run, there is a transition, in simplest terms, from "pull" to "push." Instead of flow over the lee side of the sail we have strictly "drag." The sail form that creates the most drag will push the boat fastest. Though we want to retain aerodynamic flow over the lee side as long as possible, at some point near a run it is no longer possible. After that point sail curvature is no longer helpful and "projected area" is the most important factor. Projected area is just the amount of sail area exposed to the wind. Just as a large parachute will lower a man more gently than a small one, a large sail will push the boat faster than a small one downwind. The lee telltales which have been flowing aft start to flutter as you reach this point. Easing the sail more doesn't seem to help much, and in fact will hurt your speed because you lose sail area (Figure 48B). In practicality, a spinnaker would probably be set before this point or the jib "winged" out to the other side of the boat on a pole as in Figure 48C.

The second, and even more important use, is to determine the fore and aft placement of the jib "fair lead" or "lead." On almost all sailboats, the block on either side of the boat through which the jib sheets lead is adjustable so that it can travel six inches to a foot towards the bow or stern and be locked in any spot along the track. It is this lead that determines the shape of the jib. If it is too far forward the foot of the jib is too loose and the leech too tight, because most of the pull on the jib sheet is downward. If it is too far aft, the foot is too tight and the leech too loose because of the backward pull. What we want is a compromise between the two extremes, so that the sail is not distorted. There should be an even flow of air on both sides of the sail at all levels along the luff. In other word, the sail should have a constant angle of attack to the apparent wind. If the lead is too far forward, the bottom of the sail will have a big curve in it and the lower luff will line up with the wind before the upper part does and will luff first. Conversely, if the lead is too far aft, the leech will be loose and tend to fall off up high, causing the sail to luff first at the top. So the test to determine proper jib lead placement is to head the boat up slowly until the jib begins to luff. If it luffs at the top first the lead is too far aft. If it luffs at the bottom first, it's too far forward. But if it luffs the full length of the sail all at the same time, it's set in the right spot.

The wool telltales on the jib are more sensitive to angle change than the jib itself. In other words, you can see the windward one flutter before you can see the sail start to shake along the luff. If you have three sets of these telltales, as recommended before, you can see which one flutters first and whether your jib leads are in the right place. The telltales also allow you to make the same lead judgement by watching for a stall. If the

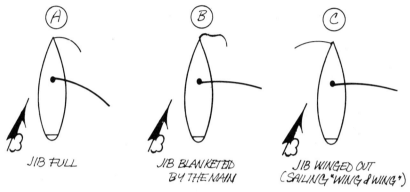

JIB FULL   JIB BLANKETED   JIB WINGED OUT
                    BY THE MAIN   (SAILING "WING & WING")

fig.48

bottom leeward one flutters first, the bottom of the sail is stalled, meaning that the sail is too flat at the bottom because the jib lead is too far aft. Thus, while racing, your crew can more readily catch a change in the situation due to an increase or decrease in wind velocity and change the jib leads fore or aft accordingly.

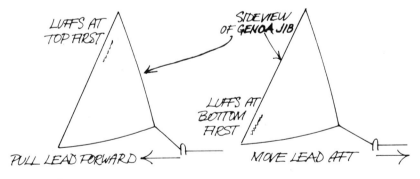

LUFFS AT TOP FIRST   SIDE VIEW OF GENOA JIB

LUFFS AT BOTTOM FIRST

PULL LEAD FORWARD ←   MOVE LEAD AFT →

fig.49

Experiment to reduce "twists" and curling of the leech to windward, so that, when pinched, jib luffs all up and down the forestay at the same time.

A Synopsis of Adjustments that can be Made to the Trim of Your Boat While Underway to Make it go Faster

Outhaul: adjusts the tension along the foot of the mainsail
    Upwind: medium -- calm day
    Downwind: loose -- any day
    Too tight: hard fold in the sail along the foot, "crow's foot" (radial
        folds stemming from the clew), wrinkles
    Too loose: puckers (small vertical fingers above the boom)

Downhaul: adjusts the tension along the luff of the mainsail
    Upwind: medium -- calm day
        taut -- breezy day
    Downwind: loose -- any day
    Too tight: hard fold in the sail along the luff
    Too loose: puckers (small horizontal wrinkles behind the mast)

Jib Cloth Downhaul (or jib halyard): adjusts tension along the jib luff
    Upwind: tight -- any day
    Downwind: loose -- any day
    Too tight: hard fold along the luff
    Too loose: "crow's feet" coming aft from the hanks

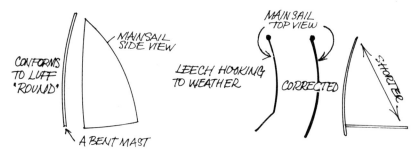

fig.50

*Adjustable Backstay: under tension – Bends mast, flattens sail and frees
    leech*
    Upwind: medium -- calm day
        tight -- breezy day
    Downwind: loose -- any day

Boom Vang: reduces "twist" by pulling down on outboard end of boom
    Breezy day: tight -- especially reaches
    Calm day: medium -- only on reaches
    Flat day with chop: tight -- only on runs

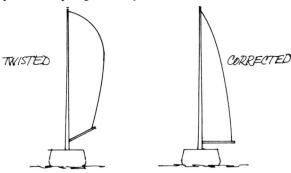

fig.51

Main Traveler: controls angle of attack of mainsail
    Upwind: in -- calm day
        out -- breezy day
    Downwind: not applicable

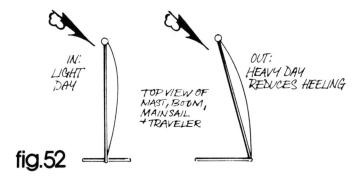

fig.52

Jib Fairleads: control angle of attack of jib and opening of "slot"
    Strong breeze: out -- reduces heeling, aft to open slot
    Light breeze: in -- point higher, forward as sheet is eased (to attain
        fullness in the sail) causing the clew to lift.

Cunningham Lines: serve as an additional downhaul when the boom is down
to the "black band," a line painted near the base of class racing boats to
limit the sail area carried. This keeps the draft moving aft in the sail on
a breezy day (see Figure 53).

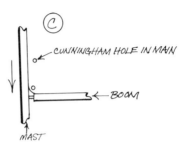

fig.53

Stopping a Sailboat

Unfortunately, a sailboat doesn't have the brakes of a car or the reverse of
a powerboat to aid it in stopping. The only way a sailboat can stop is by
heading into the wind. Sure, you can luff your sails and this will slow you
down, but you won't come to a complete stop unless you head directly
into the wind. And even when you point the boat (called "shooting" the
boat) directly into the wind, you won't come to an immediate stop but
will gradually slow down.

In order to stop alongside a man who has fallen overboard or come to a
stop with your bow at a mooring buoy, you must judge how far the boat
will shoot. Pick an imaginary spot dead downwind of your objective to be
your "turning point." The distance between this point and your objective
will vary greatly with different wind and wave conditions and with
different hull types. The stronger the wind, the shorter the distance you
can shoot. The boat stops faster because of the great resistance of the
flapping sails and the rigging to the wind and because waves are usually
higher in heavy winds and tend to stop the boat faster. In lighter airs it
will take longer for the boat to stop even though it's going slower, so allow
more room.
The approach to the turning point that allows the most flexibility is a
reach. If you approach closehauled and there's a windshift, you may have
to tack to get there. If you approach on a run, first it's difficult to judge
the turning point accurately and spin up into the wind and second, you
cannot ease the mainsail to reduce speed. On a reach, however, you have
both speed control and directional control. You can luff or trim the sails for

more or less speed and you can head up or fall off to adjust your approach to the turning point. As you round up into the wind, free the sheets and let the sails luff completely lest you back the jib accidently which forces the bow away from the wind. From the turning point to the buoy it is best not to be headed directly into the wind. Stay pointing 10°-20° towards the desired tack with sails luffing. If you miss the mooring all you need to do is trim in the sails and fall off slightly to get moving again. There is no chance of falling off accidently onto the wrong tack towards other moored boats with this method.

If you find that you have misjudged the turning point and are approaching the mooring or pier too fast, push the mainsail out against the wind. In other words, with the bow still headed into the wind, push the boom out at right angles to the boat. This is called "backing the main" and will slow the boat very quickly. As a matter of fact, if you continue to hold the boom out after the boat has stopped, the boat will start sailing backwards. Practice this. To sail well is to have complete control over the sailboat at all times. Learn how to sail the boat backwards by backing the main and jib and reverse use of the rudder. It is very satisfying to be able to make a fancy landing like rounding up into the wind to windward of a pier and backing in alongside. I wouldn't advise it without a great deal of practice, though.

Man Overboard

Should a crew member fall overboard, the first thing to do is toss him a piece of life saving equipment -- a life ring or anything that floats (and is soft in case your aim is so good you hit him). Make sure the item is not tied to the boat because you will quickly drag it out of reach of the poor person you are attempting to rescue. Next, get any sail down, such as a spinnaker, that would prevent turning the boat back. Then, if you are on a closehauled course, jibe around, aim at your turning point and shoot into the wind to come alongside (Figure 54A). The jibe is faster than a tack and takes you downwind. If you are reaching, the jibe is still faster, but you may want to play it safe and tack if it's blowing hard. If you're on a run, however, the only reasonable course is to harden up to closehauled and then tack for the turning point, as in Figure 54B. A jibe would be a useless maneuver, since you'd have to harden up anyway on the other tack. So don't believe the man that tells you one should *always* jibe to pick up a man overboard!

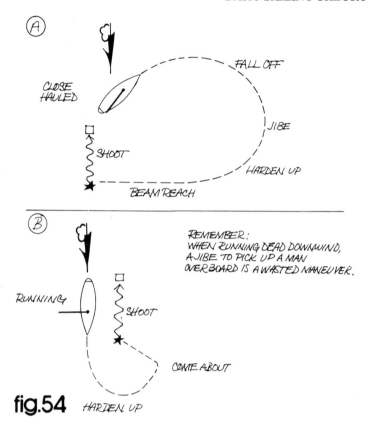

REMEMBER:
WHEN RUNNING DEAD DOWNWIND,
A JIBE TO PICK UP A MAN
OVERBOARD IS A WASTED MANEUVER.

fig.54 HARDEN UP

TEST QUESTIONS -- SECTION TWO

1. What is slot effect?
2. What is the fastest point of sailing in light air?
3. What is a header?
4. What is a lift?
5. What is the difference between a veering and a backing wind?
6. What is apparent wind?
7. Is apparent wind always stronger than the true wind?
8. What happens to the apparent wind in a puff?
9. If you head slowly into the wind and the top telltale on the jib starts to flutter on the windward side before the lower two, what does this mean to you and how do you correct it?
10. On what point of sail should you approach a mooring?
11. What should you do first if a man falls overboard?
12. Do you always jibe around to pick up a man overboard?

STABILITY

Stability is one of the most important aspects of sailing. The force of the wind in the sails of a boat tends to heel it over and without some way of counteracting this force, the boat would tip over. The greater the ability of the boat to stay upright, the more wind force she can absorb and, all else being equal, the faster she can go. However, things are never equal. If you put a heavier keel on the boat to keep it more upright, the gain you get in being able to stand up to more wind force might be offset by the increased weight of the boat which sinks the hull deeper in the water and makes it push more volume of water aside -- increased resistance from increased displacement (weight of the boat).

Weight in the keel is not the only thing that keeps the boat upright. Hull form is also a factor. A wide flat hull will have more stability than a narrow one. Imagine a raft that is six feet wide and one that is twelve feet wide. The wider raft will be able to carry more people standing on the edge without tipping over than the narrower one. As the weighted side sinks, the other side lifts out of the water, so the wider it is the more there is to be lifted out of the water. We should point out, however, the difference between "initial" and "ultimate" stability.

A flat raft has high "initial stability" because it takes a lot of weight to tip it just a little bit. But the deeper the weighted side sinks into the water the less additional weight is needed to sink it further. It will tip over very easily after it gets to a steep angle and thus has very poor "ultimate stability." A deep, narrow boat with a heavy keel may tip the first few degrees very easily, but as the keel gets lifted higher and higher by the heel angle, the more effective it becomes. So the deep keelboat may have poor "initial stability" but excellent "ultimate stability."

Stability is essentially controlled by the relationship of the position of the Center of Gravity (CG) of the boat to that of the Center of Buoyancy (CB) of the boat. The boat's CG is the center of the earth's gravitational pull on that particular boat. If the boat were suspended from a wire attached to its exact center of gravity, it could be rotated to any position and remain in that position when released. The Center of Buoyancy of the boat is really the center of gravity of all the water that the hull displaces. It is the center of all the buoyant forces pushing up on the hull. While the CG remains in one spot because the hull shape doesn't change, the CB moves in relation to what part of the hull is submerged. As the boat heels, one side submerges and the other side comes out of the water. The CB moves over further to the submerged side.

An interesting comparison results between the deep keelboat and the shallow beamy centerboarder. Figure 55A shows that at rest the CB and CG are usually in line one above another. (Crew weight plays a part in the position of the center of gravity, but we will disregard this for our purposes.) As the keelboat heels (Figure 55B) and CG moves to windward with the keel and the CB moves to leeward as the hull submerges. The greater distance the two move apart, the greater the lever-arm producing stability, with the gravitational forces pulling downward at the CG and the buoyant forces pushing upward at the CB. With the beamy centerboarder, the distance between the CG and CB is produced by the substantial lateral movement of the CB.

Figure 55C portrays the two boats flat on their sides, a rare occurrence. Note that the distance between the CB and CG of the keelboat is now the greatest it's been, whereas that of the centerboard boat has diminished. As a matter of fact, if the centerboarder tips a little further the CG will get on the other side of the CB and capsize the boat. If the keelboat tips further, it will turn right over (provided water can't get into the boat), turn turtle, and end up right side up again due to the lowness of the CG. This is called having "positive stability" -- the boat will always right itself.

Most cruising boats have self-draining cockpits, sliding hatches and hatch boards to ensure that water can't get into the boat if a freak wave flipped them over. The chances of a cruising boat turning over are slim indeed. There have been no more than two recorded incidents that I know of and one of them is doubtful. No boat is apt to turn turtle without losing it's mast due to the tremendous forces involved. One of the two indicated that the boat flipped, yet the mast was not lost, casting doubt upon the report's veracity.

Centerboarders, however, tend to capsize fairly easily so are usually limited in size to that which can be righted by the crew or at least with a minimum of outside assistance. There are some larger cruising boats that have centerboards. These boats are really keelboats in that they are self-righting (have positive stability) without use of the centerboard. The board is only used for balance and to reduce sideslipping (leeway) when sailing to windward.

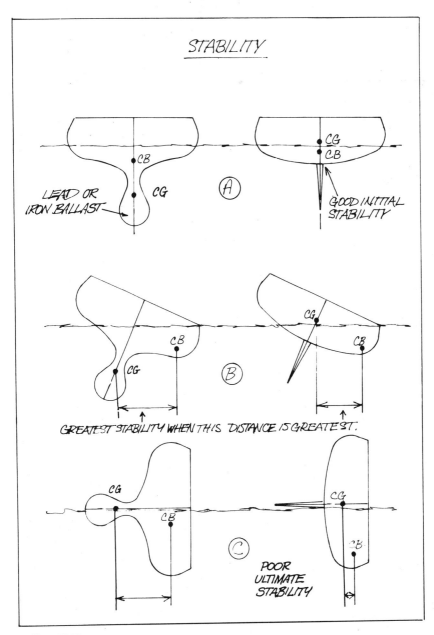

STABILITY

LEAD OR IRON BALLAST

CB

CG

(A)

CG
CB

GOOD INITIAL STABILITY

CB

CG

(B)

CG

CB

GREATEST STABILITY WHEN THIS DISTANCE IS GREATEST.

CG

CB

(C)

CG

CB

POOR ULTIMATE STABILITY

fig.55

HULL AND SAILS:
INTERRELATION IN BALANCE

Water flowing past the hull, keel and rudder of a sailboat is subject to the same basic rules as air flowing past the sails. The only difference between the sails and underwater appendages is that the latter are symmetrical while the former have the effect of being asymmetrical. But "angle of attack" (which we call "angle of incidence" for wind hitting the sails and "yaw angle" for water hitting the keel) solves the problem of getting "lift" from the keel.

Because of the pressure of the wind in the sails, a sailboat sideslips a little bit as it goes forward. This is called "making leeway." The angle between the direction that the boat is heading and an imaginary line indicating its "track" through the water is the "yaw angle" or "leeway angle" as shown in Figure 56A. Since the water has to travel a greater distance on the windward side of the keel, an area of reduced pressure results producing "lift" to windward. The more lift from the underwater surfaces, the less leeway the boat makes. In other words, it slips sideways less. Obviously, when sailing to windward we are trying to reach a destination upwind and any sideslipping that pushes us downwind is undesirable.

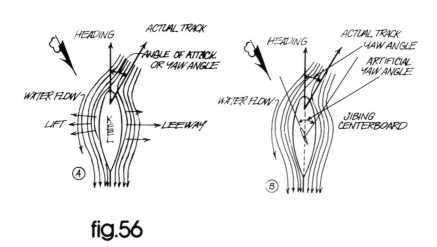

fig.56

The slower the velocity of the fluid flowing past the "airfoil" the less its efficiency as a lifting surface. So when the boat is going slowly, it sideslips more. This increases the leeway angle and, up to a point, increases the efficiency of the keel. Past that point, though, the water becomes turbulent on the windward side of the keel and a stall results. A good example of this situation is a sailboat sitting on the starting line before a race in a closehauled pointing angle but with sails luffing, waiting for the starting gun. At the gun, the crew trims in the sails to get the boat moving forward. Instead, the boat goes almost as fast sideways as she goes forward because the velocity of the water flowing past the keel is not sufficient to counteract the sideways push of the sails. The helmsman would better have sailed on a slight reach where the force of the sails is more in the direction of the boat's heading in order to pick up speed and then harden up to closehauled.

Many boats have what are called "jibing" centerboards (Figure 56B). This means that they can be angled towards the wind to produce an artificial yaw angle. The idea is to set the centerboard as if the boat were side-slipping in order to make a larger angle of attack to the water and reduce leeway. An added advantage is that the hull, which creates a great deal of drag if going sideways through the water, is headed more in the direction of the boat's track. Only the centerboard, the effective lifting surface, is cocked to windward. At high boat speeds, though, the skipper must be careful about cocking the centerboard too much because stalling will result. Just like the sail, where the airflow can't bend around a large curvature at high speed, the water is less able to bend around a centerboard with a large angle of attack the faster the boat sails.

The sails of a boat sailing upwind create a forward and sideways force. The keel or centerboard resists the sideways force. Unfortunately, due to drag, they also resist the forward force. But to get into that opens a whole Pandora's box of how to reduce "form" drag, "frictional" drag, and the hull's "wave-making" drag, which is really a subject for a book on naval architecture, not practical sailing.

Balance

In order to sail properly, and certainly to race successfully, one must take the "balance" of the boat in consideration. By "balance" we mean the tendency of the boat's heading to either deviate or to remain straight when the helmsman releases the tiller or wheel. If he lets go of the tiller and the boat turns away from the wind, to leeward, it is said to have "lee helm."

Conversely, if the boat turns to windward it has "weather helm." If it sails straight ahead, the boat is perfectly balanced.

Though the above can be used as a guideline, be careful not to be misled by "artificial" weather helm. A boat will normally turn into the wind when the tiller is released because of the forces acting on the rudder. As water flows past the windward side of a rudder, "lift" is generated due to the angle of attack with the water flow. If the rudder post (which turns the rudder) is located on the leading edge of the rudder and attached to the trailing edge of the keel, all the area aft of the post is pulling to windward, thus tending to turn the boat into the wind. Since the water flow has traveled the full length of the keel to reach the rudder, though, the flow is not very effective as a lift factor.

Separated or "spade" rudders have become increasingly popular on cruising boats recently. The rudder is placed near the stern of the boat where it has the greatest leverage for steering. It is a lifting surface in itself, and since it isn't attached to the keel and is meeting fairly non-turbulent water, such a rudder is very efficient. These rudders usually are "balanced" in that the rudder post enters the rudder about one-fourth of the way back rather than being attached along the leading edge. Hopefully then, the center of the pull to windward will be right at the post and the rudder will remain straight. This reduces artificial weather helm. It also decreases true weather helm because the rudder, as a lifting surface, pulls the stern of the boat to windward to a small extent.

Excessive leeway also causes artificial weather helm. Take an extreme example of a boat slipping straight sideways through the water and making no forward motion. The water on the leeward side of the rudder aft of the rudder post pushes the rudder to windward giving the appearance of weather helm.

The way one can distinguish the artificial from the true weather helm is if the rudder has to be deflected from straight ahead in order to make the boat sail straight. In other words, if the tiller is being held constantly a few degrees to windward to make the boat sail straight, there is a true weather helm.

I've sailed on cruising boats with balanced spade rudders that the owners swore sailed fastest with a "neutral" helm, and that once they developed a slight weather helm the boat slowed down. My observation was that though the helm felt neutral (there was no tug on it because the rudder post entered the rudder well aft of its leading edge) there was indeed a

slight weather helm because the tiller was being held to windward a few
degrees. When the weather helm developed to a point where the helmsman
could feel it, the tiller was being held to windward at an angle large enough
to increase rudder drag, thus slowing the boat down.

In most boats sailing to windward a little weather helm is desirable. Where
the rudder is attached to the trailing edge of the keel, as in Figures 57A
and B, it is obvious that the couple of degrees of rudder needed to
counteract a slight weather helm tends to give the keel "lift" and reduce
leeway. Too much weather helm, however, will just cause turbulence and
drag as in Figure 57C.

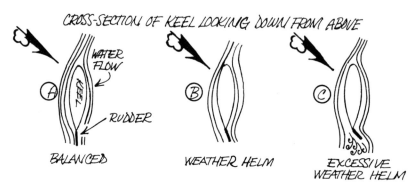

CROSS-SECTION OF KEEL LOOKING DOWN FROM ABOVE

WATER FLOW

KEEL

RUDDER

Ⓐ BALANCED   Ⓑ WEATHER HELM   Ⓒ EXCESSIVE WEATHER HELM

fig.57

The same holds true with the spade rudder, which gets its lift from the
angle of attack the rudder makes with the water. A little weather helm
cocks the rudder to windward and increases the angle of attack just like
the "jibing centerboard" mentioned earlier.

There are many reasons for weather or lee helm, but foremost is the relationship between the "Center of Effort" of the sail plan and the "Center
of Lateral Resistance" of the hull shape. Imagine a sailboat drifting sideways down a river with the current. It hangs up on a tree stump under the
surface. At all locations *except one* on the underwater body of the boat
it would pivot off the end of the stump and continue downstream. If it
hangs up at that one spot, it will remain on the end of the stump in
balance even with the current hitting the other side of the boat. This point
is called the "Center of Lateral Resistance" of the boat, or CLR.

By geometrically determining the point that is the combined center of all the sails that are set on the boat, we can find the "Center of Effort," or CE of the boat. This is the center of all the forces acting to push the boat sideways against the center of all the forces resisting that push, the CLR.

Now imagine the boat as if it were a weather vane on top of a roof pivoting on the CLR. If the CE is directly above the CLR, the boat is in balance. So if the wind blows on this weather vane, it won't pivot.

However, by placing more sail area towards the bow of the boat, the CE moves forward. When it is forward of the CLR the tendency is for the bow of the boat to be blown to leeward. If you move the CE aft of the CLR by placing more sail area near the stern of the boat, the boat pivots to windward.

SAILBOAT WEATHERVANE

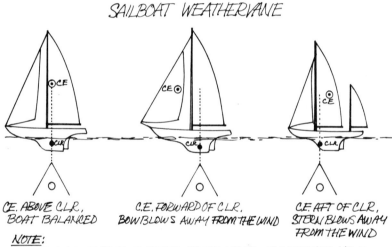

CE. ABOVE CLR,
BOAT BALANCED

C.E. FORWARD OF CLR,
BOW BLOWS AWAY FROM THE WIND

CE. AFT OF CLR,
STERN BLOWS AWAY
FROM THE WIND

NOTE:
THIS IS AN OVERSIMPLIFICATION SINCE NAVAL ARCHITECTS HAVE
FOUND THAT A BOAT NEEDS TO BE DESIGNED WITH THE C.E. A
CERTAIN AMOUNT FORWARD OF THE CLR, TO BALANCE THE BOAT,

fig.58

The easiest way, in theory, to change the balance of a boat would be to move the sail area forward or aft. If you move the mast (and along with it, the main and jib) aft, you increase weather helm, and if you move the rig forward you reduce weather helm or increase lee helm. Since most boats have varying amounts of weather helm and rarely have lee helm, any change that results in lee helm is usually just a reduction in weather helm for most boats and we tend to state it that way.

In practice, moving the whole rig fore and aft can be time consuming on a small boat and well-nigh impossible on a large one without extensive carpentry. A solution is to change the amount of sail forward or aft. A friend of mine had a yawl which never seemed to develop any weather helm, so he replaced the mizzen mast with a larger one, bought a new mizzen and at long last achieved weather helm. Another friend owns a sloop that constantly developed too much weather helm. When nothing else seemed to work, he put a bowsprit on the boat and bought a larger genoa with the desired results. The former brought the CE aft to achieve weather helm, while the latter brought the CE forward to reduce it.

Obviously, if changing the amount of sail area fore or aft changes the balance of the boat, changing the efficiency of the sails will have the same effect. If you sail without a jib your boat will have a strong weather helm from the mainsail and if you sail under jib alone the boat will have a strong lee helm. If you luff the mainsail, thereby reducing its efficiency, the CE moves forward with a corresponding reduction of weather helm. If you luff the jib, you will increase weather helm.

By careful adjustment of the main and jib we can steer a fairly accurate course without even touching the tiller. This is good practice because one never knows when a rudder might fall off or a tiller break. One time we lost a rudder in the middle of a Transatlantic Race and steered the last 1000 miles by adjusting the sails alone. For a closehauled course, trim the jib fairly flat and then play the mainsheet -- luffing the main to head off and trimming it to head up.

On a small boat the distribution of your crew weight will have an effect on balance. When a boat heels the bow wave on the lee side becomes larger (Figure 59) and tends to shove the bow to windward.

fig.59

Also, the center of effort (CE) is out over the water (Figures 60A and 60B). Imagine a sailboat in a dead flat calm with the mainsail and boom way out over the water as if it were running free. If you come along in an outboard motorboat and push the end of the boom in the direction that the boat is pointing, the boat will turn away from you (into the imaginary wind). The reason, of course, is that the push is out on a lever arm, at the other end of which is the drag of the hull. So, you can see that *additional* weather helm develops when the center of effort is out over the water when you are reaching, running or heeling.

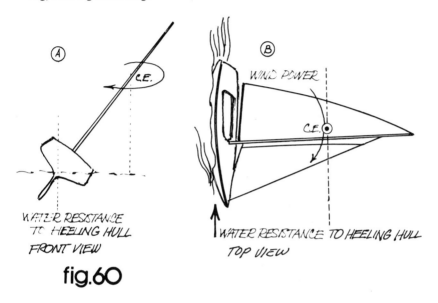

fig.60

By shifting the crew weight from one side of the boat to the other, a small sailboat can be steered without using the rudder if the breeze is light enough.

The center of effort can be moved in a few other more subtle ways. If a mast is raked aft the sail area is moved aft. Raking a mast means leaning it, and is not to be confused with bending it. To lean it aft, the headstay is eased and the backstay is tightened.

Sail shape also has a great deal of effect on balance. For instance, if the mainsail has a tight leech (one in which the batten ends are pulled slightly inboard, to windward) weather helm will be increased.

Another way to change the balance of the boat is to leave the center of effort in one place and move the center of lateral resistance forward or aft. Since the CLR is the center of the underwater lateral plane of the boat, the only way (without a centerboard) to move it is to submerse less or more of the boat. If you depress the bow of the boat by moving crew or equipment forward, the CLR moves forward and weather helm increases. The opposite results if you depress the stern, allowing the bow to lift higher out of the water. Imagine the bow being blown to leeward by the wind as more of it is exposed. This is only a memory aid and not the cause of the lee helm.

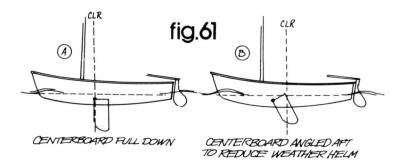

CLR

fig.61

CLR

Ⓐ   Ⓑ

CENTERBOARD FULL DOWN   CENTERBOARD ANGLED AFT
                                           TO REDUCE WEATHER HELM

Sailboats that have centerboards can move the CLR more easily. Since a centerboard pivots on a forward pin it describes an arc as it is lowered. Thus the area is further aft when the board is halfway down (angled aft) than in its full down position (vertical under the pin). So to move the CLR aft, just raise the board partway if it's all the way down or lower it partway if it's fully housed in the centerboard trunk (all the way up). This will have the effect of reducing weather helm.

A well designed boat will have a slight weather helm which increases as the wind velocity increases. The weather helm creates "lift" for the rudder, and also gives the helmsman some "feel" for the boat. The slight tug allows the helmsman to ease his pressure on the tiller in order to let the boat come up closer to the wind. He increases his pressure on the tiller to get the boat to fall off away from the wind. In other words, he is steering only one direction, while the boat steers itself the other direction. A boat is very difficult to steer well if it has to be steered up towards the wind as well as away from the wind. It is said to have no "feel."

Another reason it is desirable to have some weather helm is the fact that with weather helm the boat will automatically head up in the puffs. This reduces heeling and maintains the angle that the wind originally made with the sails, because the apparent wind comes aft in puffs. For the latter reason, even in light air, one should head up in the puffs.

To reduce excessive weather helm, you can (1) add more sail area forward, (2) reduce sail area or sail effectiveness aft, (3) move the mast forward, (4) reduce mast rake, (5) move crew or equipment aft, (6) reduce heeling by hiking or (7) place the centerboard in the halfway down position.

HULL SPEED

Generally, the larger the boat, the faster it can go. For a displacement boat, a heavy deep-keel boat, the maximum speed a given hull can attain from wind power is called "hull speed" and is largely dependent on the waterline length of the boat. Hull speed is expressed as $1.34\sqrt{LWL}$. If a cruising sailboat has a waterline length of 36 feet, she should be able to sail 1.34 x 6, or approximately eight knots.

The idea behind this is that a boat cannot travel faster than the wave she creates and the speed of a wave is $1.34\sqrt{\ell}$, "ℓ" being the distance between the crests. The length, "ℓ", of a wave increases proportionally as the height ("h") of the wave increases. So the higher the wave, the greater the distance between crests and the faster it travels. This relates to the sailboat in that as the sailboat's speed increases, the greater the volume of water the bow has to push aside and the larger the bow wave becomes. As the bow wave increases in height, the distance between its crest and that of the wave following it, the quarter wave, increases until it approaches the waterline length of the boat itself. This can be noted as the sailboat in Figures 62B and 62C picks up speed. At first there are numerous small "transverse" waves while the boat travels slowly. These spread out as the bow wave increases in height until, in Figure 62D, hull speed is attained and there are only two waves along the hull, the bow wave and the quarter wave. To push a boat past its theoretical hull speed, though possible, would take more power in wind and sails than most boats can withstand. A beautiful example of hull speed can be seen whenever a tugboat is cruising to a job. They have trememdous power and very easily reach hull speed. The classical wave pattern of a bow wave and quarter wave is always present at that speed. For a tugboat to go even marginally faster would take so much more power it would be uneconomical.

When a boat does exceed its hull speed, as the one being towed in Figure 62E, the stern tends to leave the quarter wave behind and drop into the trough between waves. The bow rides high in the air. Often one sees a number of displacement one-design racing sailboats being towed to a regatta at greater than hull speed. Their sterns are practically under the water.

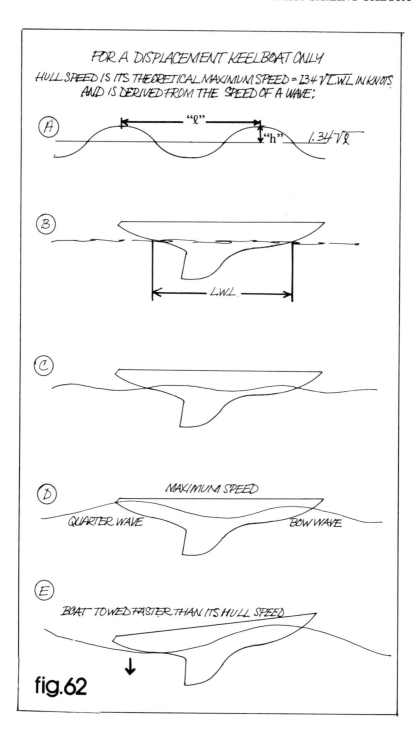

FOR A DISPLACEMENT KEELBOAT ONLY

HULL SPEED IS ITS THEORETICAL MAXIMUM SPEED = 1.34 √L.W.L IN KNOTS.
AND IS DERIVED FROM THE SPEED OF A WAVE:

Ⓐ "ℓ" "h" 1.34 √ℓ

Ⓑ L.W.L.

Ⓒ

Ⓓ MAXIMUM SPEED
QUARTER WAVE   BOW WAVE

Ⓔ BOAT TOWED FASTER THAN ITS HULL SPEED

fig.62

Note that we keep reiterating "displacement" in reference to hull speed. The flat bottom centerboarder and many fin-keeled boats really don't have a hull speed. They are technically "planing" boats. A planing boat skims along the surface of the water like a skipping stone rather than plowing the water aside. Usually it has a v-shaped hull near the bow and a fairly flat bottom aft. As its speed increases the bow rides up on the bow wave and finally the boat levels off at planing speed with the bow wave well aft. Most powerboats, particularly in the 30 foot range, act this way. At lower speeds the boat plows through the water. Then as the speed increases and the bow wave moves aft, the bow rises up in the air. At a certain speed the unsupported bow, with the bow wave well aft, levels off as the boat breaks into a high speed plane. For a sailboat, its ability to plane or not depends on its length/weight ratio. If it's too heavy for its length it will never be able to plane.

There is a way that a displacement boat can exceed its theoretical hull speed, and that is by "surfing." Surfing is being pushed by a wave just the way surfers ride a wave on a surfboard. In large wave conditions, when running downwind, a sailboat can get on the front side of a wave and carry it for quite a number of seconds with a tremendous burst of speed. It takes good helmsmanship to be able to get on the wave just right to reap the greatest benefits from it. Though light planing boats tend to surf more easily, displacement boats are perfectly capable of surfing and can far exceed their hull speed in this manner.

RIGHT OF WAY

Power Versus Power

Quite often beginners feel that their sailboat always has right of way over powerboats even when running the engine. Not so. Only when a sailboat is not running its engine is it classified as a sailboat. So even if you have a day sailor with a tiny outboard motor, when the motor is running (even if the sails are set) you are liable to the motorboat "rules of the road" (as the right of way rules are called).

Though there are many minor ramifications, the main thing to remember when motorboats are on a converging collision course is that the one in the other's "danger zone" has the right of way. The "danger zone" of a motorboat is from dead ahead to two points abaft the starboard beam. If there is any boat approaching from that area you must avoid it. It is the "privileged" vessel in that it has the right of way, and you are the "burdened" vessel in that you must keep clear. The obligation of the privileged vessel is to hold its course and speed so you won't be misled in your attempts to keep clear. What must be avoided at all costs is the kind of mixup that occasionally happens to pedestrians going in opposite directions on a city street. One steps one way just as the other decides to pass on that side, then changes direction only to find the other changing the same way. On a boat this could bring about a serious collision, so the privileged vessel *must* maintain her course until it is obvious that a collision is imminent, at which time she must avoid it.

If two boats are approaching each other from dead ahead, both should turn to starboard. If one is approaching the other from any point aft of the danger zone, he is overtaking and must keep clear of the overtaken boat.

Power Versus Sail

The above should be enough basic information to keep you out of trouble when you are running your engine and meet another powerboat. Another set of rules applies when you are sailing and meet a power boat. Many people have the misconception that a sailboat always has right of way over a motorboat. Though this is usually true there are a number of exceptions when a sailboat doesn't have rights: When the motorboat is anchored or disabled, is being overtaken by the sailboat or, when the motorboat is a commercial vessel with limited maneuverability in a narrow channel.

Sail Versus Sail

There are only three basic possibilities when your sailboat approaches another: (1) You are on the same tack as the other boat, (2) you are on opposite tacks or (3) one of the boats is overtaking the other.

For this reason there are three basic rules to cover the three possibilities: (1) On the same tack, the leeward boat has right of way, (2) on opposite tacks, the starboard tack boat has right of way and (3) if overtaking, the boat ahead (the overtaken boat) has right of way.

There are three sets of general rules used by United States yachtsmen: the International Rules, the Inland Rules and the Racing Rules. The International Rules were formed back in the days of square-rigged sailing ships. These ships were much more maneuverable downwind than when close-hauled, so the right of way was given to any boat that was closehauled over any boat running free. In all other situations the first three basic rules mentioned above applied. Because of the gray area between closehauled and a close reach, and between running free and a broad reach, the inadequacy of this rule has long been recognized. It wasn't until 1965 that it was dropped from the International Rules leaving only the three basic rules. Due to U. S. governmental red tape, the Inland Rules, which previously agreed practically verbatim with the International Rules, have not yet been changed. This leaves us with one conflict between the rules: If a closehauled boat on the port tack is approaching a boat running free on the starboard tack, under International Rules the starboard tack boat has right of way. But under the Inland Rules the closehauled boat is the privileged boat. Since the two rules apply in different waters, this conflict shouldn't make too much difference -- unless there was indecision between skippers as to whether they were in International or Inland waters. The Coast Guard's "Rules of the Road" lists a number of "imaginary lines" drawn to and from various lightships, lighthouses, light towers and points of land along the coast outside of which are International waters and inside of which are Inland waters. The "three mile limit" has nothing to do with the Rules of the Road.

For instance, near the tip of Long Island in New York, there is an island called Block Island. If you sail from Long Island Sound and circumnavigate Block Island, you sail from Inland waters into International waters and back into Inland waters again. So the International Rules are of more concern to the sailor than he might expect and he should be aware of which rule he is under at all times.

The basic Racing Rules agree with the three basic International Rules with one exception: the overtaking rule is in effect but the opposite tack rule overrides it if the situation arises. For example, (1) a port tack boat keeps clear of another port tack boat it is overtaking, (2) a port tack boat keeps clear of a starboard tack boat it is overtaking, but (3) a starboard tack boat doesn't have to keep clear of a port tack boat it is overtaking. This could only occur on a dead run and the defense for the port tack boat is to flip over to starboard.

TEST QUESTIONS -- SECTION THREE

1. Describe positive stability.
2. What is yaw angle?
3. What is a balanced rudder?
4. Why is excessive weather helm detrimental?
5. How do you reduce weather helm?
6. How do you steer without a rudder?
7. Define Center of Effort.
8. Define Center of Lateral Resistance.
9. Describe hull speed.
10. Describe planing.
11. Describe surfing.
12. In the following situations, determine which boat has the right of way under each rule -- International, Inland and Racing.

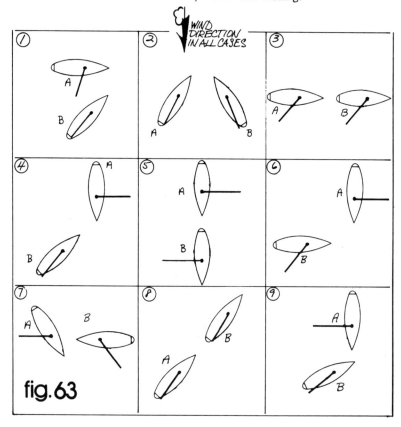

fig. 63

HEAVY WEATHER

Though we advise beginners to sail only on pleasant days, after you have gained some confidence in your abilities try sailing on progressively windier days.

I know an owner of a cruising boat who races. Every spring he picks the windiest day he can find to go out and practice. The result is that he gains complete confidence in his boat, equipment and crew. If you can handle so much wind, any less windy day is a breeze (pardon the pun).

Until you either sail in a great deal of wind or get caught out in a passing squall you won't have confidence in your ability to handle the boat in a heavy wind situation. The best way to put your mind at rest is to imagine the worst that can happen -- capsizing, man overboard or loss of the mast. None of these three is so frightening. If you are sailing a centerboarder, practice capsizing and righting the boat. After capsizing, swim the bow of the boat around into the wind so the wind can get under the sails and separate them from the water as the boat comes up. Then stand on the centerboard to apply righting leverage to the boat, scramble in when it's upright and bail it out or sail it dry if it has venturi bailers or transom flaps.

Practice man overboard by tossing out a cushion and seeing how fast you can retrieve it, making sure to bring the boat to a complete stop.

You can't practice loss of the mast, but you can be prepared for that eventuality. An anchor with plenty of line, a paddle and a first-aid kit would help put your mind at ease. On a larger boat, wire cutters would be a good idea for cutting away a mast that might be damaging the hull.

Once you are confident that there is nothing that could happen to you or the boat that you can't handle, then all the rest is just sound and fury. It's natural to be a bit apprehensive or frightened of heavy winds at first, but

93

soon you'll find that you actually enjoy the heavy stuff -- an exciting part of sailing!

When you get caught in your first squall remember that the most important thing to do is shorten sail. You may see the squall approaching and get some sail down before it hits if it looks bad enough, though it's hard to judge without a great deal of experience just how bad a squall will be. Sometimes a nasty looking sky turns out to be only dark clouds and rain, but no more wind. However, when a bad squall hits, the wind can go from 10 mph to 40 or 50 mph in seconds. If you hadn't reduced sail previously, you should have at least prepared for the possibility of having to. Halyards should be neatly coiled and ready to run. Each crew member should be briefed as to what his responsibilities will be if the squall is a bad one so not a second is lost in giving orders. This has a secondary advantage of decreasing the chance of panic. When the first blast hits and the boat is laid over on its side, the brain processes of even some experienced crew members tend to become stupefied. If he knows what he is expected to do beforehand, he doesn't have to think.

On a small boat, the mainsail usually has greater sail area than the jib and should be the first sail to lower. If it isn't lowered, as the wind increases the skipper should release the mainsheet to reduce heeling. The boat, due to the weight of the wind and sea, will probably be on more of a close reach than closehauled. At some point, even with the main and jib luffing completely, the wind force will be sufficient to lay the boat over on its side. The boom and mainsail will hit the water to leeward which, due to the boat's forward motion, will force the sail in towards the center of the boat just at a time when you want to let it out. The drag on the end of the boom pivots the boat to leeward just when you want to head up into the wind. The mainsail fills and over you go if it's a capsizable boat. So lower the mainsail first! The boat should sail well under jib alone.

If it's still blowing too hard, lower all sails and run before the wind "under bare poles" (no sail), unless there's a chance of running aground.

Your best friend in bad conditions may very well be your anchor. If the visibility is down to a few feet, you're not sure of your position and you're afraid you may be blown ashore, get your anchor over the side. You may not have enough line to reach bottom, but you can be fairly sure that the anchor will hook before you get into water shallow enough for your boat to go aground, or be swamped by breakers.

On a cruising boat, the genoa often has much more sail area than the main. If you're caught with the genoa up in a squall, that's the sail you should lower. The cruising boat has better stability than the small centerboarder, so there is no need to worry about dipping the main boom. The boat should sail well under main alone until you can put on a storm jib, and the main can usually be reefed if necessary.

ANCHORING

After you've learned to sail, it probably won't be long before you do some cruising. You'll sail along some coast putting into little harbors at night. When choosing a spot to anchor make sure it's in sheltered water, not in a channel, and check the chart to determine that there's enough water for your boat in that location at low tide. Then choose a spot with enough room to swing around your anchor without hitting other anchored boats. Boats of the same type will swing about the same way. For instance, a deep-keeled sailboat will line up more with the current while a shallow draft powerboat with high superstructure will line up more with the wind. Drive past a harbor and sometimes you will see the sailboats pointing in one direction and the powerboats in another. So, if you anchor among other boats, make sure you are closer to the ones that are similar to yours.

Next get the anchor out on deck, coil the anchor line so it will run free, and secure the bitter end. Many anchors have been lost because the end hasn't been tied and the man feeding out the line gets to the end before he expects to. It can happen easily at night when, because of an increase in wind velocity, a crew member lets out more line to improve the holding power of the anchor and doesn't realize the end wasn't tied until it's too late.

Allow the boat to coast to a complete stop at the point where you want to be and toss the anchor over the side making sure the line doesn't get tangled in the flukes as it goes. It's supposed to be bad practice to toss the anchor rather than lower it over the side, but everybody does it and as long as the anchor is light and you're careful to avoid the line tangling it isn't all that bad. As the boat starts to drift backwards, feed out line until about 5 to 1 "scope" is attained. This means you have let out five times as much line as the depth of the water. If the water were 20 feet deep, you would have let out about 100 feet of line. A scope of four or five to one should be adequate in most cases where the bottom is good for holding and there's not much wind or you're anchoring for a short time. Increase the scope if there's a lot of wind or you want to be sure you won't drag. The smaller the angle the anchor line makes with the bottom, the greater the holding power of the anchor because the line will be pulling the anchor along the bottom rather than lifting it off the bottom. When you feel you have eased out sufficient scope, snub the anchor line around a cleat so that the momentum of the boat will jerk the anchor home much like one jerks a fishing line to sink the hook into the fish's mouth. Check that you're not dragging by pulling on the line and, from time to time, by glancing at your relationship with points on shore and with other boats.

The next morning when you want to leave, reverse the process. If you have an engine, power along the anchor line towards the anchor with the man in the bow overhauling (gathering in) the slack line. When the bow of the boat is directly above the anchor, again snub the line on a cleat and let the momentum of the boat break the anchor free. If the anchor is still stuck, give your boat a little more power and try pulling from different directions in hopes of rotating the anchor. Remember that sailboats have powerful winches that can be used as an aid. Also, if the seas are heavy, as the bow goes down take in any slack in the anchor line and snub it. Then, as the bow rises on the next wave, the buoyancy of the boat may break free the anchor. To be successful with this method, you will probably have to take in the slack on a number of waves before you have it all.

DOCKING

Under sail, docking isn't much different from picking up a man overboard or a mooring. The boat has to be headed into the wind to stop. If the wind direction is parallel to the dock, (Figure 64A) just shoot the boat into the wind and come to a stop parallel to and alongside the dock. If the wind is blowing away from the dock and towards the water (Figure 64B), shooting into the wind takes you straight into the dock. If you're going too fast remember you can back your main to slow down. Approaching at an angle would be better than approaching head on. Avoid coming in perfectly parallel to the dock if the wind is blowing out from it, because when you luff the sails to slow down you will start drifting sideways away from the dock, unless it's a long one and a crew member can hop onto the dock with a line before the boat slows down too much.

If the wind is blowing perpendicular to the dock and towards it from the water, docking is more difficult. The best approach is without any sail up if the wind is heavy or with only the jib if the wind is light. So round up into the wind to windward of the dock as in Figure 64C and lower the sails. Then drift into the dock. You'd be surprised how well some boats can sail without any sail up. A Soling, for instance, will sail practically on a beam reach without sail once it has picked up some speed.

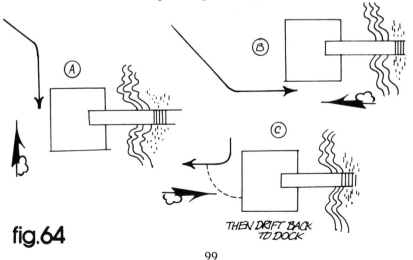

THEN DRIFT BACK
TO DOCK

fig.64

If you have a cruising sailboat you will probably power into the dock. Generally, the same rules apply as with sail but you have more flexibility. If possible, approach the dock upwind and/or upcurrent depending on the force of each. The one most common mistake is approaching too fast. The cruising sailboat has a great deal of momentum and is hard to stop. It usually has a small two-bladed propeller hidden behind the keel. The result is that you can put the engine in reverse, rev it up and the boat still moves forward, gradually slowing down. I knew a man who had a beautiful 48-foot sailboat with a Mercedes diesel as auxiliary power. He always approached the dock too fast. About 100 yards away he'd be going five knots, put the engine in reverse and hope that the boat would come to a stop by the time it was alongside. One day, when there was a 60-foot yacht on the far end of the dock, sticking out at right angles to the long side that my friend planned to approach, he misjudged the speed. Even though the engine was screaming in reverse we were now alongside the dock with about two knots of headway and heading straight for the bow section of the other yacht extending past the edge of the dock end. My friend couldn't steer out because the stern would just bump if he tried to make such a sharp turn. Luckily I was able to toss a bow line to the other boat's owner who ran aft and snubbed it around a piling. Our bow crunched into the dock as the boat's forward motion was checked just short of a collision.

A line tied aft from the bow is one of the common lines used in tying a boat up at a dock. It's called a "forward spring" line and keeps the boat from moving forward. An "after spring" line runs from the stern to a point forward on the dock and keeps the boat from drifting backwards. These spring lines combine with the bow and stern lines to keep the boat parallel to the dock so it will rest on fenders and not rub its topsides on the dock or on pilings.

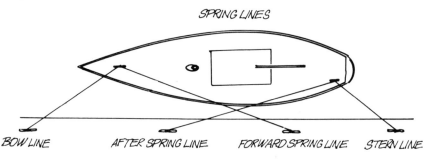

SPRING LINES

BOW LINE   AFTER SPRING LINE   FORWARD SPRING LINE   STERN LINE

fig.64 d

NAVIGATION

It's not our purpose here to delve very deeply into coastal navigation or "piloting" as it is commonly called. We just want you to be able to plot a course that avoids hazards.

Compass Variation

Our chief navigational aid is the compass. There are various errors one must be aware of. First the compass does not point to the North Pole (true north) but rather to a magnetic mass (magnetic north). The difference between the direction the compass is pointing and true north is called *Variation.* It changes according to geographical location, as shown on your chart. Printed on the chart is a "compass rose." North on the outer rose is true, while north on the inner rose is magnetic. Since the inner rose already has taken variation into account, as long as we use the inner rose for plotting our courses, we can forget about having to compute variation. Since we are using a magnetic compass, magnetic directions are all we care about and can be taken right off the chart. There's no reason to get a true course first and then convert to magnetic by applying variation, though this over-complicated process is still used by many people.

Compass Deviation

Deviation is a more subtle form of compass error. Magnetic portions of the boat itself tend to affect the compass. On a sailboat, though, after the compass has been checked and adjusted, deviation rarely amounts to more than one degree. Since you can't steer anywhere near that close, it's not worth worrying about. Again, just be aware that deviation exists. If you want to check your compass to make sure that the compass isn't way off, pick two points such as landmarks or buoys (though the latter are not as accurate as a lighthouse), compute the course between these points on a chart, and run between them. The course shown on your compass should be the same as the one you computed. Run in four directions, north, south, east and west, because the deviation could be small going north and large going the opposite direction. You will probably find that on a sailboat the error is negligible particularly if you are sailing on a small body of water with relatively short distances between the buoys you'd be using for navigation. A five degree error in heading for a course between two buoys a mile apart means you can still practically touch the second buoy when you come abeam or it. However, if you were steering a course for twenty miles, the five degree error would make a substantial difference on your final location. Don't let me lull you into carelessness, though. Accuracy is a habit one should foster when navigating. You never know when you'll be caught in a dense fog and need all the accuracy you can muster.

Chart Distances

The vertical chart lines are *meridians,* or "degrees of longitude" which point to the North and South Poles on a globe, but are parallel when spread out on the "Mercator projection" (the one we use for most of our coastal navigation).   The horizontal lines are *parallels,* "degrees of latitude."   There are sixty minutes to a degree; thus each minute of latitude (and longitude, at the equator) equals one nautical mile. To measure distance we can use the gradations along the side edges of the chart.   In many cases each mile so shown is divided into tenths for accuracy and ease in measuring distance. If you want to know how far it is between two buoys, place one point of a set of dividers on one buoy and spread them so that the other point is on the other buoy. Then move them to the edge of the chart and see how many minutes fall within the points. If the distance was seven minutes, that converts to seven nautical miles. If you are traveling 3.5 knots (a knot is one nautical mile in one hour so never say "3.5 knots per hour" because that's like saying "3.5 miles per hour per hour") then you will cover that distance in two hours.

Plotting a Course

When we draw a course line on a chart, we want to know the magnetic direction of the line because it represents our boat moving on a compass course. The compass rose on the chart represents the boat's compass pointing to magnetic north. What we'd like to do is move the compass rose over, place it on our course line and read our course off it as if it were the boat's compass. Since the rose is printed on the chart, we can't do it that way, so we have to do the next best thing -- move the course line over to the compass rose. To accomplish this we use an instrument called a "parallel ruler" or "parallel rules," a dandy nautical gadget for carrying a line from one chart position to another, exactly parallel to the original line so that its direction will remain the same.

Lay the edge of your parallel rulers along the desired course. Press down on one leg and move the other out in the direction of the nearest compass rose. Then press that one down and move the first in parallel. Alternately, press-spread, press-spread the legs of the ruler until you have centered one edge of the parallel ruler right over the cross in the center of the compass rose. Then read, under the magnetic rose, the course in degrees.

Four mistakes are commonly made by beginners: (1) letting the parallel rulers slip so that they are no longer parallel to the course line, (2) reading the course off the outside (true) rose rather than the inside (magnetic) one, (3) reading the wrong increment (the smaller roses have increments of two degrees while on the larger ones every degree is marked) and (4) reading off the wrong edge of the circle -- in other words, reading 270 degrees (west) when you're actually traveling 90 degrees (east).

Chart Reading

Buoys are marked on the chart as small diamonds with a dot underneath to indicate their exact location. The color of the diamond, usually red or black, corresponds to the color of the buoy. The most common ones are "nuns" and "cans." Nuns are red, conical and even numbered. Cans are black, cylindrical and odd numbered. Next to the diamond on the chart will be, for example, N"4", so you know that it's a nun with the number "4" painted on it. Or it might read C"3" to indicate a can buoy painted with the number "3".

If the dot under the diamond is in the center of a small purplish circle it means the buoy is lighted. The characteristics of the light are written alongside. "Fl R 3 sec" means it's a flashing red light going on every three seconds. "FG" would mean "fixed green." A note such as "60 FT 13 M" would mean that the light is sixty feet above the surface of the water and has a visibility of 13 miles.

Study a chart and familiarize yourself with the various other abbreviations. The colors on a chart are important. White areas are deep water, light blue is under 20 feet deep and green is out of the water at low tide. Check how the depth is indicated. On most U.S. charts the depths are in feet at mean low water. Also, there are contour lines at certain constant depths, so you can get the idea of the bottom contour.

Remember the time-honored navigational byword: "Red...Right...Returning," which means that red buoys are left to starboard when entering a harbor or when sailing from a larger body of water into a smaller one.

Bearings

Navigation on a sailboat is slightly complicated by the fact that we can't always steer the course we want -- if our destination is dead upwind, for example. On a powerboat we could plot all our courses the night before and run the preset courses allowing for current and drift. But with a sailboat we are mainly keeping track of our location as we sail along and adjusting our course to the desired destination accordingly.

One of the best methods of determining your position is by taking bearings. Sight over your compass at two or three lights or landmarks and record your bearing to each in degrees. For each one, locate the same number on the nearest magnetic rose (inner circle) on the chart. Place an outside edge of your parallel rules on both this number and the cross in the very center of the rose. Work the other outside edge of the parallel rules along the chart to the landmark (that you took the bearing on) and draw a line through it -- extending the line out into the water. You are located somewhere along this line. Now repeat the process using the bearings you had for the second and third landmarks or lights. Taking three bearings will give you a triangle when plotted, which is a bit more accurate than the cross you get from only two bearings. If the triangle is too large you should take your bearings again because one was probably inaccurate. Ideally, you would want all three to cross at exactly one point -- your position -- but that rarely happens.

When you choose the lights or landmarks, try to pick ones that are quite a distance from each other. If you are using only two bearings your greatest accuracy would be from two that were 90 degrees apart from your position. Figure 65 shows bearings taken with a 5 degree error in each. Note that using landmarks A and B produces a much larger aggregate error than using A and C which are farther apart.

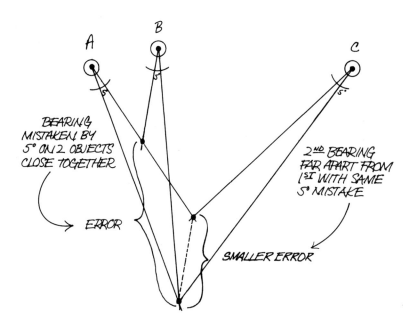

fig.65

SPINNAKER

We will conclude these lessons with a fast basic rundown of spinnaker work, for those beginners, and there are always a few, who instinctively master the essentials of sailing early, and thirst for the delight (and extra work) of sailing under this most picturesque of sails.

The spinnaker is like a large parachute that pulls the boat downwind. It can be set with the true wind direction anywhere from dead astern to about abeam. It's made of light nylon and adds so much sail area to the total sail plan of the boat that speed is markedly increased when a spinnaker is set.

Refer to Figure 66 and learn the various lines involved with spinnaker work. The spinnaker is hoisted by the spinnaker halyard. One corner is held in place by the spinnaker pole which is always set to windward opposite the main boom. The corner attached to the pole is the tack of the spinnaker and attached to it is the spinnaker "after guy" or more commonly, "guy." The free corner of the spinnaker has a sheet attached to it like any other sail. The only tricky thing about the foregoing terminology is that during a jibe, the pole is switched over to the new windward side and the old guy becomes the new sheet (attached to the free corner of the sail) and the old sheet becomes the new guy (running through the jaws in the end of the pole).

There are two lines to hold the pole in position -- the topping lift to keep it from falling when the spinnaker isn't full of wind, and the foreguy (some people call it the spinnaker pole downhaul) to keep the pole from "skying" (pointing way up in the air) when the spinnaker is full.

TYPICAL SPINNAKER RIG

HEAD

KC 100

TOPPING LIFT

CLEW   SPINNAKER POLE   TACK

SPINNAKER GUY

FOREGUY

SPINNAKER SHEET

fig.66

Courtesy of Abbot Boat Works

Preparation for Setting the Spinnaker

Starting at the head of the spinnaker, run down both edges one at a time folding each accordion-style, holding the folds in one hand as you go. This will ensure that the spinnaker isn't twisted. If two edges are untwisted the third one, the foot in this case, also has to be straight.

Then, holding onto the folded edges and all three corners of the sail, stuff it into whatever container the boat uses to set the spinnaker from. This used to be called a "turtle" because it was originally a plywood board covered with black inner tube rubber with an opening at one end. When the spinnaker was stuffed in it, with the three corners hanging out the open end, and placed on the foredeck of the boat near the bow, it looked like a turtle. This term has been carried over even though spinnakers are now stuffed into bags, buckets or even cardboard boxes.

The halyard, sheet and guy are then connected to the three corners. Make sure the halyard is attached to the head of the sail -- the corner with the swivel. Since the spinnaker is vertically symmetrical, you can attach the sheet and guy to either of the other two corners. Make sure the sheet and guy are outside of everything on the boat (shrouds, stays, etc.) before connecting them.

In the case of a Soling or larger boat, the spinnaker is usually set on the leeward side. In smaller boats, where there is danger of capsizing if a crew member goes to the leeward side of the boat, the spinnaker is set to windward and pulled around the jibstay.

Next, set up the pole to windward with the guy running through the outboard end.

The Hoist

The key to a good set is to separate the lower corners of the spinnaker as the halyard is being raised. Often this means cleating the sheet and pulling the tack of the sail out to the pole as quickly as possible with the guy, unless you have enough crew to have a man on the sheet also. The halyard should be pulled up smartly so the spinnaker will neither fall overboard in the water nor will fill with air before it's all the way up. If the latter happens the halyard man may have difficulty holding on unless he gets a wrap around a winch or cleat in a hurry.

The Set

There are a few simple rules that form a good foundation for basic spinnaker work: (1) Set the pole at right angles to the apparent wind. Use the masthead fly since it's in less disturbed air than the shroud telltales and make sure the pole lies perpendicular to it.

(2) Since the spinnaker is a symmetrical sail, it should look symmetrical. Neither corner should be higher than the other. If the clew is higher than the tack, the pole should be raised to even them out.

(3) The pole should be perpendicular to the mast so it will hold the tack of the spinnaker as far away from the blanketing effect of the mainsail as possible. If the pole needs to be raised, as in rule #2, don't just pull the topping lift (which raises only the outboard end), but raise the inboard end also if it's adjustable.

(4) Ease the sheet until a curl appears along the luff of the "chute" (short for parachute spinnaker, as it was formerly called) and then trim it back until the curl disappears. The spinnaker trimmer will have to watch the luff of the spinnaker constantly, because the moment he looks away the chute will collapse, almost as if it were waiting for him to look away.

If you follow these few basic rules you shouldn't have any trouble learning to fly a spinnaker.

The Jibe

There are two basic types of jibes: the "end for end" jibe used on small boats with light spinnaker poles and the "dip-pole" jibe used on larger boats when the pole is heavy.

We'll concern ourselves with the former since it is applicable to the type of boat most learn on. The man on the foredeck stands behind the pole facing forward. Just before the jibe he disconnects the pole end from the mast and, as the boat turns downwind, he grabs the sheet and snaps the jaw of the pole over it. Then he passes the pole across the boat, unsnaps the other end from the old guy and snaps it into the eye on the mast. Meanwhile, the man in the cockpit is easing the sheet and trimming the guy as the boat turns into a jibe. This keeps the spinnaker downwind and full of air. The skipper pulls the main across and, if it is blowing hard, after the boom crosses the centerline, he turns the boat back downwind to keep it from broaching (rounding up broadside to the wind) which it has a tendency to do after a jibe.

The Douse

Taking a spinnaker down is much like running a movie of the hoist backwards. First grab the sheet as near the clew as possible and pull it into the cockpit so the spinnaker will come down behind the mainsail. Second, let the guy run free and start gathering in the foot of the sail. Third, lower the halyard fairly fast, but not so fast that you get ahead of the man gathering it in lest the sail falls in the water.

TEST QUESTIONS -- SECTION FOUR

1. On a small boat, which sail do you lower first in a squall?
2. Define scope.
3. Name some ways to raise a stuck anchor?
4. Describe spring lines.
5. Describe variation.
6. Describe deviation.
7. What distance is represented by two minutes of latitude?
8. What are four common mistakes made in plotting a course?
9. What does "Red Right Returning" mean?
10. List the steps involved in the spinnaker hoist, set and douse.

APPENDIX I

1. When boarding, step in the middle of the boat (on floorboards, not on the seat), holding onto the shrouds if possible and immediately lower the centerboard, if there is one.

2. Hank on the jib, tack first, feeding it between your legs for control.

3. Check along the foot for twists. Reave and attach the jib sheets. Tie stop knot in end. Attach jib halyard after checking for twists.

4. Feed the foot of the mainsail along the boom. Attach the tack, the clew, then pull the foot tight with the clew outhaul.

5. Put the battens in the batten pockets, starting with the lowest, with the most flexible ones highest up, thin end in first, hole end in last.

6. Follow along the luff to remove twists and feed the luff onto the mast starting at the head. Attach main halyard.

7. Attach rudder and tiller, if necessary.

8. Make sure the mainsheet is completely free to run, check halyard for twists, raise the main.

9. Take out the boom crutch (if any) as the main is being raised and hold the boom up by hand.

10. Make sure the leech of the main isn't caught under a spreader as the sail is raised.

11. Secure and coil the main halyard. You can use a half-hitch here, but not on sheets.

12. Pull the main downhaul tight if there is one.

13. Raise and secure the jib.

14. Untie the mooring line, but hold onto it. Back the jib to the desired tack and drop the mooring.

15. Don't cleat the mainsheet on a small boat in a breeze.

16. When checking the sail trim, adjust the jib first. Ease it until it luffs, then trim it in. Next, do the same with the main.

17. For extra speed raise the centerboard when on a run. When jibing have it partway down. To windward on a breezy day have it partway up to reduce weather helm.

18. Man overboard -- PRACTICE THIS!
     a) Toss life preserver or floating cushion to him.
     b) If closehauled or on a reach, jibe and shoot into the wind alongside the man.
     c) If on a run, harden up to closehauled, tack, and shoot for him.

19. Capsize:
     a) STAY WITH THE BOAT until help arrives! DON'T try to swim for shore.
     b) Try to lower the sails, so righting the boat will be easier.
     c) If the boat is small enough, point the bow to the wind and stand on the centerboard to right it.

APPENDIX II

PARTS OF THE BOAT

1. *Port and Starboard Side* -- Facing toward the bow of the boat, the port side is on your left and the starboard side is on your right.

2. *Beam* -- The widest part of the boat.

3. *Length Overall* -- The length of the hull between extremities (not including bowsprit).

4. *Waterline Length* -- The straight-line distance between the point where the bow emerges from the water and the point where the stern emerges from the water.

5. *Draft* -- The distance from the waterline to the lowest part of the boat.

6. *Topsides* -- The sides of the boat between the waterline and the deck.

7. *Aft* -- Near the stern, behind, in back.

8. *Tiller* -- A stick attached to the rudder for steering.

9. *Rudder* -- A flat, hinged board near the stern that deflects the passing water one way or the other to change the boat's direction.

10. *Cockpit* -- The part of the boat that is not decked over.

11. *Standing Rigging* -- All the permanent wires that hold the mast up. Broken down into two categories:
    a. *Stays* -- that keep the mast from falling toward the bow or stern.

b. *Shrouds* -- that keep the mast from falling over the port or starboard side (upper and lower shrouds).

12. *Running Rigging* -- All movable rigging mainly:
   a. *Halyards* -- The wires (and/or ropes) that pull the sails up. They are attached to the sails with *shackles* (u-shaped fittings).
   Never -- let go of the end of a halyard. It will begin to swing in the breeze and slide its way up to the top of the mast.
   Always -- make sure that both ends of a halyard are attached to something.
   b. *Sheets* -- The lines with which you trim the sails. The mainsheet is led through a series of *blocks* (pulleys) to your hand or a *cam cleat*. It controls the swing of the boom, in or out. The jibsheets are attached to the clew of the jib. They are led, one on either side of the mast, through the *fairleads* (eyes or blocks on a track), around a *winch* (cylindrical drum increasing your mechanical advantage) to your hand or cam cleat. The jib is almost always trimmed on the *leeward* side (where the boom is) of the boat. Stop knots should be tied in the end of the jibsheets.

13. Others:
   Outhaul: The rope (and/or wire) that attaches the clew of the mainsail to the outboard end of the boom. It is used to adjust the tension along the foot of the mainsail. Taut, for a flat sail: sailing upwind and/or on a breezy day. Loose, for a baggy sail: sailing downwind and/or on a calm day.
   Downhaul: The *tackle* (rope and blocks) that holds down the inboard end of the boom. It is used to adjust the tension along the luff of the mainsail. Just like the outhaul: taut, for a flat sail -- upwind and/or breezy. Loose, for a baggy sail -- downwind and/or calm.

14. *Spreaders* -- Crossbars on the mast to spread the angle the shrouds make with the mast and thereby increase their leverage.

15. *Telltales* -- The short pieces of yarn attached to the shrouds and the backstay. They show how the wind is striking the boat. The helmsman must constantly be checking the telltales on the *windward* side (the side of the boat that the wind is coming over). They indicate how the sails should be trimmed.

APPENDIX III

SAILING TERMS

1. *Windward* -- The direction *from* which the wind is blowing.

2. *Leeward* -- The direction *to* which the wind is blowing.

3. *Port and Starboard Tack* -- Opposite to the side the mainsail is on. If the mainsail is on the starboard side, the boat is on the port tack and vice-versa.

4. *To Tack* -- To change from the port tack to the starboard tack (or vice-versa) turning the bow of the boat into the wind. The command of preparation is "Ready About." The command of execution is "Hard Alee."

5. *To Jibe* -- To change from the port tack to the starboard tack (or vice-versa) turning the bow of the boat away from the wind (downwind). The command of preparation is "Prepare to Jibe" and the command of execution is "Jibe Ho." Imagine yourself on a boat. Face the wind. If you turn the boat so the bow swings through the direction you're facing, it's a tack. If you turn the boat the other way, it's a jibe. Remember the two "T's" -- *T*ack *T*owards (the wind).

6. *A Beat, To Beat, Beating* -- A series of tacks.

7. *Points of Sailing* -- Describing the direction of the boat in relation to the direction of the wind.
   a. *Closehauled* -- About 45 degrees from the wind.
   b. *Reach* -- About 90 degrees from the wind. Wind is "abeam."
   c. *Run* -- About 180 degrees from the wind. You are sailing "downwind."

8. *By the Lee* -- If the boat has been turned too far downwind, so that the wind is now coming over the same side of the boat that the main boom is on, you are sailing "by the lee." Risky.

9. *In Irons* -- When the boat is headed into the wind and has lost all forward motion it is "in irons." The rudder will no longer turn the boat (unless it is drifting backwards), since it works only by deflecting the passing water.

10. *True Wind* -- The actual direction the wind is blowing.

11. *Apparent Wind* -- The vector (change in wind direction) produced by the boat's forward speed.

12. *Weather Helm* -- The tendency of a boat to head into the wind if the helm is dropped.

13. *Lee Helm* -- The tendency of a boat to head away from the wind if the helm is dropped.

14. *A Header* -- A change in wind direction towards the bow of the boat.

15. *A Lift* -- A change in wind direction towards the stern of the boat. Remember that a header for a boat on the port tack is a lift for a boat on the starboard tack.

16. *Veering* -- A change in wind direction clockwise in relation to the compass. Northeast to East, for example.

17. *Backing* -- A change in wind direction counter-clockwise in relation to the compass. West to Southwest, for example.

18. *Bernouli's Principle* -- Simply that if the velocity of the air flowing past one side of an airfoil is greater than that on the other side, the pressure correspondingly decreases on the former side creating a suction like that which creates the lift of an airplane's wing and the pull of a boat's sail.

19. *Slot Effect* -- The funneling of air behind the mainsail through the slot formed between the main and the jib. This increases the velocity of the air on the lee side of the main, thereby increasing its suction and efficiency.

20. *Backwind* -- Caused by the slot being too narrow and forcing the funneled air into the backside of the main, rather than past it. Backwind makes the main appear to be luffing.

21. *Surfing* -- Being pushed by the motion of the wave, much like a surfboarder.

22. *Planing* -- Increased speed by skimming along the surface of the water. Depends upon the shape of the hull and the boat weight. Most keel boats cannot plane.

23. *Stability* -- The relation of the center of buoyancy to the center of gravity. The further apart they are, the greater the stability.

24. *Positive or Ultimate Stability* -- The boat with positive stability will always, like a cat, end right-side-up (unless she fills with water). Most cruising boats have positive stability, can be closed up tight so no water can enter, and have self-bailing cockpits.

25. *Hull Speed* -- The theoretical speed beyond which a displacement boat cannot go, usually $1.34\sqrt{LWL}$.

26. *Collision Course* -- If the relative bearing of the two converging yachts doesn't change, eventually they will collide.

APPENDIX IV

PROPER SAIL FOLDING

1. Fold foot over window.

2. With one hand anchoring cloth, reach upsail with the other.

3. Lifting and dragging the head toward you,

4. Fold it down over the window and foot.

5. Continue with these accordion-like folds,

6. Lifting and pulling the sail toward . . .

7. The growing pile of folds,

8. Until the head is reached.

9. Then roll up the pile in big folds,

10. Starting so the clew will be outside on a mainsail,

11. Tack outside on jib, and you will be . . .

12. All ready for tomorrow's sail.

APPENDIX V

ADDITIONAL KNOTS

Clove Hitch

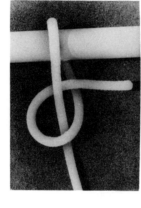

1. Around and over itself, around and under itself,

2. And you have a Clove Hitch

Two-Half Hitches

1. Around and through,

2. And around and through.

122

Rolling Hitch

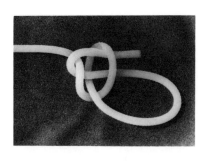

1. Try this one,

2. You'll like it . . .

Fast Bowline

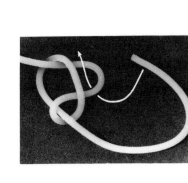

1. Feed free end through,

2. And pull the loop out . . .

3. Presto: a quick bowline.

123